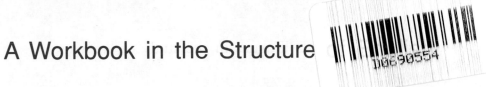

A Workbook in the Structure

For all my colleagues in the study of language

A
Workbook
in
the Structure
of English

Linguistic Principles
and
Language Acquisition

William Rutherford
University of Southern California

Copyright © William Rutherford, 1998

The right of William Rutherford to be identified as author of this work has been
asserted in accordance with the Copyright, Designs and Patents Act 1988.

First published 1998

2 4 6 8 10 9 7 5 3 1

Blackwell Publishers Inc.
350 Main Street
Malden, Massachusetts 02148
USA

Blackwell Publishers Ltd
108 Cowley Road
Oxford OX4 1JF
UK

ISBN 0–631–20479–2 (pbk.)

British Library Cataloguing in Publication Data

A CIP catalogue record for this book is available from the
British Library.

Typeset in 10 on 12 pt Sabon
by Graphicraft Typesetters Ltd., Hong Kong
Printed in Great Britain by T. J. International Ltd., Padstow, Cornwall

This book is printed on acid-free paper

Contents

Part II   Grammatical Operations   97

Part III   Grammatical Relations

Part V   Other Areas   323

Acknowledgments

The genesis of the *Workbook* has benefited greatly from commentary provided by many of our colleagues and representing interest areas as diverse as the material itself. I owe the largest debt of thanks to Hiroyuki Oshita (USC), who somehow found time during the writing of his doctoral dissertation to work extremely carefully through the entire manuscript and comment extensively and insightfully on everything from level ordering to unaccusatives to the theory of functional categories. My sincere thanks go also to Bernard Comrie (USC), Stephen Franks (Indiana University), and Roland Hinterholzl (USC) for immensely helpful extended commentary on a great deal of the material. For very helpful and detailed suggestions concerning more specific areas of the book I wish to express my gratitude to Kathleen Bardovi-Harlig (Indiana University), Audrey Li (USC), Trevor Shanklin (Northern Arizona University), Larry Selinker (University of London), and Helmut Zobl (Carleton University). For other valuable commentary, I am grateful to Gerald Berent (Rochester Institute of Technology), Lynne Eubank (University of North Texas), Suzanne Flynn (MIT), Susan Foster-Cohen (British Institute Paris), Noel Houck (Temple University Japan), Eric Kellerman (University of Nijmegen), Tom Roeper (University of Massachusetts, Amherst), and Paul Schachter (UCLA). I also owe a great deal to the students at USC who took the various courses in which I have used portions of the *Workbook* during its long development and whose reactions, ranging at times from excitement to skepticism to occasional horror, I would not have traded for anything.

Finally, I wish to offer my thanks to the editorial staff at Blackwell Publishers who handled the manuscript at different stages in its development: Mary Riso (Development Editor), Linda Auld (Desk Editor), Fiona Sewell (freelance editor), and especially Steve Smith, whose services as Commissioning Editor have proven indispensable for the publication of this work.

Permissions Acknowledgments

Assignment 10: Code-switching data from Woolford (1983: 527) reprinted with permission of The Massachusetts Institute of Technology.

Assignment 68: Data from Nishigauchi and Roeper (1987: 99) reprinted with kind permission of Kluwer Academic Publishers, and of the author.

Assignment 69: Data from Zobl (1984: 205) reprinted with permission of John Benjamins Publishing Company.

Assignment 75: Data from Rutherford (1989: 178–179), copyright Cambridge University Press 1989. Reprinted with the permission of Cambridge University Press.

Assignment 81: Data from Wenzell (1989: 77, 79–80) reprinted with permission of Ablex Publishing Corporation.

Assignment 82: Data from Kumpf (1984) reprinted with permission of the author.

Assignment 85: Data from Wenzell (1989: 77, 79–80) reprinted with permission of Ablex Publishing Corporation.

Assignment 96: Examples from Finer (1991: 354–355) reprinted with permission of John Benjamins Publishing Company.

Assignment 113: Data from Order of acquisition vs. dynamic paradigm: A comparision of method in interlanguage research, by Thom Huebner. *TESOL Quarterly*, *13*, 21–28. Copyright 1979 by Teachers of English to Speakers of Other Lanuguages, Inc. Excerpts from pp. 25–26 adapted with permission, and with permission of the author.

Assignment 144: Examples from Clark (1974: 317–323) reprinted with permission of the Lingusitic Society of America and of the author.

Introduction

A Workbook in the Structure of English is designed to serve as major course material for graduate or high undergraduate programs whose principal focus is the syntactic, morphologic, and semantic structure of the English language. The workbook aspect of the material is of crucial importance, since what is to be learned from the study of language is accomplished more effectively through the DOING of linguistics than through merely reading about it or listening to someone talk about it. The *Workbook*'s subtitle – *Linguistic Principles and Language Acquisition* – reflects two kinds of catalyst for optimal absorption of the wide range of information about English to be worked on: Tying such information, wherever possible, to known principles of linguistics (e.g. of grammatical theory, of semantic interpretation, of language processing, etc.) provides the necessary means for beginning to understand much of the vastness of the language as being to a considerable extent all of a piece, so to speak. Showing how a lot of such information, together with its underlying principles, figures in the remarkable feat of language acquisition both in childhood and in adulthood serves to "bring the language to life," to choose an expression whose ambiguity is, under the circumstances, quite apt.

If an appreciation of the structural regularities of English can be enhanced through an understanding of how they instantiate the more general principles of linguistics and of what their great relevance is to acquisition phenomena, then there is opportunity for such appreciation to cut both ways. More than once has it been said that one cannot have a theory of how something is acquired without a theory of what that something is. In the case of language acquisition, that "something" is of course language itself. Yet in many academic programs containing a language acquisition component the language side gets short shrift. One more reason for creating a workbook of this kind is therefore the need to give serious attention to the development of linguistic knowledge and to the importance of such knowledge for understanding the burgeoning language acquisition research literature that presupposes it. But linguistic knowledge does not exist apart from knowledge of some specific language or languages. Because English is by far the language that has figured most often and most prominently in the literature, and because study of its structure forms the core of so many academic language programs, it is English structure as the embodiment of linguistic principles and English as the target of acquisition, in childhood as well as adulthood, that is the focus of attention and the object of study throughout this material.

A Workbook in the Structure of English is designed to be used by itself, although one may also wish to make use of it in conjunction with some other text that treats certain areas of English study in more depth than is possible in a workbook with a great range of material. The task of compiling a work with this kind of breadth has led to important decisions as to how the material should be arranged, what theoretical linguistic stances the facts of English might reflect, what prior language knowledge (if any) to presuppose on the part of the user, and in what ways maximum cohesion throughout such a wide array of material can be achieved. In a sense, the way in which the material has been arranged follows quite logically from a decision to let the major aspects of theoretical underpinning be drawn from generative linguistics, with language typology, language function, and language processing figuring in a somewhat lesser, though still very important, theoretical role. But the decision to give prominence to the generative approach has in turn followed logically from a decision to relate the body of knowledge about English wherever possible to findings in the growing quantity of acquisition research literature, whose chosen grammatical model is for the most part the generative one. Some of the needed cohesion attempted in the *Workbook* thus derives automatically from an implicational chain that comes full circle:

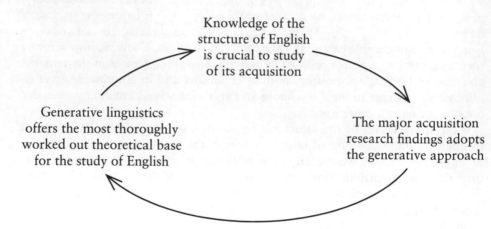

Knowledge of the
structure of English
is crucial to study
of its acquisition

Generative linguistics
offers the most thoroughly
worked out theoretical base
for the study of English

The major acquisition
research findings adopts
the generative approach

Making up the *Workbook* are 168 problem-solving tasks, labeled "assignments". This material is organized into a short preliminary part and five main parts, each subdivided into sections, the assignment numbers running consecutively across the parts. The five main parts are labeled as follows: (I) Grammatical Constructs and Configurations, (II) Grammatical Operations, (III) Grammatical Relations, (IV) Typology, and (V) Other Areas (including word formation). The task-oriented, problem-solving format has been deliberately chosen as the best means for inculcating the ability to think like a linguist in developing the requisite analytical skills. Problem-solving as a learning device – more specifically as a search through a problem space – has some amount of research to support it. Gabrys, Weiner, and Lesgold (1993), to cite just one example, compare it to other instructional methods such as direct instruction, observing a model, studying examples, and discovery learning, and have this to say:

> it is expected that the student who learns through problem solving will retain more, because problem solving engages the student's active, generative, cognitive processes; that the knowledge acquired will be useful, rather than "inert", because the conditions of possible use would be similar to the conditions of learning; and that the knowledge might be flexible, adaptable to similar new situations, because in the course of problem solving the learner has built up knowledge of the set of alternative possibilities in the problem area. (1993: 120)

The value of all this in the linguistic realm is in development of the user's analytical skills – mediated through the structure of English – which can also be regarded as an engagement necessarily prior to that of theory building. The value of all this in the acquisition realm is in development of the ability to read and understand the linguistics-based acquisition research literature. The symbiotic relationship between the two – English linguistics and acquisition – can thus find reinforcement through careful consideration of the learning procedures by which they are assimilated.

Other major features of the *Workbook* are the following:

- The material is conceived in such a way that it may be engaged initially by any user having a small prior acquaintance with some basic language concepts.

- The assumed acquaintance would cover such things as the various parts of speech, the notion of what constitutes a language unit or constituent, the fact that there are different "levels" of analysis (phonology, morphology, syntax, semantics, etc.), the idea of surface ambiguity pointing to underlying structural contrast, the idea that surface differences can mask underlying similarities, and so on. The eight assignments appearing in the introductory section, "Preliminary Material," are conceived for the purpose of revisiting these concepts, should this be deemed useful.

- Textual material provides background and context for each of the assignments to the extent that is called for.

- It will be noted that in all but a few instances any one assignment takes up no more than one or two pages. It is assumed that the pages will be tear-out, to facilitate handing in and grading of assignments.

- Individual assignments are graded in terms of level of difficulty and the degree indicated by means of a star or stars (*) following the assignment number –*, **, or ***– and ranging from easy (*) to rather challenging (***).

- Many of the individual assignments are interrelated in one of three different ways: (1) assignments may appear in small clusters, wherein each builds upon material treated in its predecessor; (2) an assignment appearing in one part of the book may take a different tack on material appearing in another part; (3) an assignment may feature further development of material introduced in an earlier section. There is thus extensive cross-referencing throughout the book.

- The content of the assignments in almost all cases represents closed-end activity. That is, there is a presumed "correct" or "appropriate" response, though in a number of cases different theoretical considerations might lead to modified outcomes.

- The effort to construct mostly problem-solving tasks of the closed-end variety is motivated by a desire (1) to make these activities more quickly and easily gradable, (2) thereby to enable more of them to be undertaken, and (3) thus to ensure that the student encounters the widest possible range of English linguistics phenomena.

- The *Workbook* is accompanied by an *Instructor's Manual* (on disc) containing suggested solutions to the assignments, extended discussion of the solutions wherever it might be called for, and guidelines for use of the material in a variety of instructional settings.

Preliminary Material

Name: _____   Date: __ / __ / __   Class: _____

<hr>

ASSIGNMENT
A*

Grammatical Category
and Part of Speech

Using the following passage, cite ONE example of the categories listed below:

If linguists try to write a description of English which can be fed into the computer for use in translating Russian, they will want an extremely specific one.

1. noun *computer*
2. verbal noun [i.e. noun derived from a verb]
3. adjective
4. adverb
5. preposition
6. (modal) auxiliary
7. article (determiner), definite
8. article (determiner), indefinite
9. pronoun
10. subordinator (introducing a subordinate clause)
11. infinitive
12. relative pronoun
13. past participle
14. gerund
15. passive
16. main (finite) verb
17. prepositional phrase
18. noun phrase
19. relative clause
20. proper noun

ASSIGNMENT **Word Analysis**
B*

The distinction traditionally drawn between **inflectional** and **derivational** affixes is covered in most introductory linguistics texts. The distinguishing characteristics are in general the following:

	DERIVATIONAL	INFLECTIONAL
Grammatical category of the stem:	Changed *hate / hatred* [V]　　[N] *imp / impish* [N]　　[ADJ]	No change *hat / hats* [N]　　[N] *limp / limped* [V]　　[V]
Position within the word:	Closer to stem *arguments* *stabilized*	Word-final *arguments* *stabilized*
Quantity permissible within the word:	One or more *compute* *computer* *computerize* *computerization*	Only one *compute* *computed* *computing* **computeding* **computinged*
Productivity:	Limited *hatred* **hateness* *bossy* **bossish* **bossly* *impish* **impy* **imply* *friendly* **friendy* **friendish*	Virtually unlimited *hatreds* *bossed* *imps* *friendlier*

(continued)

Name: _____ Date: __ / __ / __ Class: _____

Analyze the English words below using the following format:

	STEM	DERIVATIONAL AFFIXES	INFLECTIONAL AFFIXES
taste	*taste*		
tastes	*taste*		-*s*
tasty	*taste*	-*y*	
tastier	*taste*	-*y*	-*er*

1. tastiness
2. relationships
3. cravings
4. analyzability
5. person
6. personal
7. personalities
8. desertization
9. parliamentarianism
10. advise
11. advises
12. advisor
13. advisee
14. children
15. mitten
16. smitten
17. toiler
18. taller
19. broken
20. broadened

ASSIGNMENT C* **Constituency (I)**

Crucial to all forms of linguistic analysis is the notion of **constituency** – i.e. whether or not a particular group of words functions as a UNIT. Tests for constituency include whether or not the group can move, whether it can take a pronoun substitute, whether it can be questioned with a wh- word, whether it can be deleted, and so on. Using such tests, determine whether or not the *italicized* elements in the following sentences are constituents.

		Yes	No
1.	Somebody put sugar *in his coffee*	✓	...
2.	*Somebody* put sugar in his coffee	...	...
3.	*Somebody put sugar* in his coffee	...	...
4.	Somebody *put sugar in* his coffee	...	...
5.	The prisoner *escaped*	...	...
6.	The *prisoner escaped*	...	...
7.	There's a rumor *that he saw a ghost* circulating	...	...
8.	The rumor *that he saw a ghost* is circulating	...	...
9.	That he saw *it is possible*	...	...
10.	That section's reserved for old *men and women*	...	...
11.	That section's reserved for *old men* and women	...	...
12.	You don't need to *put up with that*	...	...
13.	You don't need to put *up with that*	...	...
14.	You don't need to *put up with* that	...	...
15.	Everybody's *been wonderful to us*	...	...
16.	Everybody's been *wonderful to us*	...	...
17.	Everybody's been *wonderful* to us	...	...
18.	*We did do* it	...	...
19.	*We did* do it	...	...
20.	We did *do it*	...	...

ASSIGNMENT D* Constituency (II)

So-called **question tags** serve to turn statements into questions. The **tag** in English contains the tense-carrier or modal from the statement, a pronoun whose antecedent is the subject of the statement, and reversed-negative polarity. For example:

George won't come, will he?

statement   tag

For each of the following sentences, construct an appropriate question tag. Then underline the pronoun and the constituent in the statement serving as its antecedent and connect the two with a line. For example:

George won't come, will he?

1. The guests have already arrived,

2. In the summer you have to water often,

3. A lot of the people are here,

4. There are a lot of people here,

5. Whatever he does is OK with you,

6. You don't think much of it,

7. That problem there will probably be no solution for,

8. For there to be nobody here would be strange,

9. I look like I've seen a ghost,

10. It's been blowing up a storm out there,

ASSIGNMENT E* Underlying and Surface Structure

Attention is drawn in this exercise to superficial similarities and fundamental differences among pairs of sentences. In each of the following sets of three seemingly similar sentences only two have similar underlying structures. Simply identify the one sentence in each set whose underlying structure feels somehow "different." In thinking about where the differences might lie, employ a variety of diagnostics like the following:

- **constituency** (whether or not a group of words functions as a unit)
- **inversion** (e.g. inverting the two halves of the sentence)
- **deletion** (i.e. of a constituent)
- **passive/active correspondence** (i.e. converting one into the other)
- **references for anaphoric elements** (e.g. pronouns), etc.

Bear in mind, however, that although any one of these diagnostics may be sufficient for our purposes, not every one of them is always necessary. Consider, for example, a set like this:

(a) *She knew the answer to the question*
(b) *She knew the answer in a second*
(c) *She knew the answer to our knowledge*

Application of some of the above diagnostics would yield results like the following:

Inversion and constituency:

*To the question she knew the answer
In a second she knew the answer
To our knowledge she knew the answer

Active/passive and constituency:

The answer to the question was known
?The answer in a second was known
?The answer to our knowledge was known

(continued)

These tests perhaps corroborate the feeling that the odd member of this set of three seems to be (a).

Employ similar reasoning in following up your feelings about the following:

1. (a) *It's a game he never wins*
   (b) *It's a shame he never plays*
   (c) *It's a paper he never reads*   . . . . .

2. (a) *The tree was planted near a hill*
   (b) *The tree was planted by a well*
   (c) *The tree was planted by a workman*   . . . . .

3. (a) *The first bus to take will be no. 5*
   (b) *The first bus to arrive will be no. 5*
   (c) *The first bus to board will be no. 5*   . . . . .

4. (a) *She made him what he is today*
   (b) *She made him a pair of socks*
   (c) *She made him a nervous wreck*   . . . . .

5. (a) *He set the teapot on the shelf*
   (b) *He left the teapot in the sink*
   (c) *He broke the teapot in the kitchen*   . . . . .

6. (a) *This car drives smoothly*
   (b) *This shirt irons neatly*
   (c) *This rock fell suddenly*   . . . . .

7. (a) *Her hobby is costing money*
   (b) *Her hobby is playing poker*
   (c) *Her hobby is collecting stamps*   . . . . .

8. (a) *They had a meal to eat*
   (b) *They had a reason to eat*
   (c) *They had nothing to eat*   . . . . .

9. (a) *I promised him to help*
   (b) *I wanted him to help*
   (c) *I allowed him to help*   . . . . .

10. (a) *What he wants is none of your business*
    (b) *What he wants is all of your business*
    (c) *What he wants is some of your business*   . . . . .

Name: _____   Date: __ / __ / __   Class: _____

ASSIGNMENT **III-Formedness**
F*

The sentences listed below are thought to deviate from standard English usage in some way, for special effect. Most have been lifted from advertisements in the print media, a few from other sources. What is the nature of these deviations – i.e. syntactic, morphological, lexical, semantic, processing, etc.?

1. *America is on the improve!* (ad.: home repair products)

2. *Great oaks from little acorns grow.* (old saying)

3. *They do make movies like this anymore.* (ad.: movie)

4. *Accessorize your system.* (ad.: audio/video equipment)

5. *His performance got him a standing ovulation.* (news item)

6. *More seat vs. more seats.* (ad.: airline)

7. *There are words that appear in the dictionary that no one knows where they came from.* (article in consumer magazine)

8. [Electric razor brand] *announces a new discovery that obsoletes the wet shave.* (ad.: electric razor)

9. *You're invited to President Aristide's home-going!* (newsletter)

10. *When I look in the mirror, I see a totally new me.* (ad.: weight-loss clinic)

11. *Gifts for the home to please everybody at prices to please your pocketbook and terms to please your budget!* (ad.: store)

12. *British Caledonia. The airline airlines hate.* (ad.)

13. *It's as thrilling as it's bloody!* (ad.: movie)

14. *That's a place where the hand of man has never set foot* (overheard)

15. [Brand] *chicken and turkey makes a great sandwiches.* (ad.: luncheon meats; picture of foot-high sandwich)

16. *Beefeater. The most gifted gin.* (ad.)

17. *Please send me a coupon good for . . . I have enclosed the inner seal from any size jar of* [brand]. (rebate offer, instant coffee)

(continued)

18. *Suddenly the fastest way to Europe is also the comfortablest.* (ad.: airline)

19. *Your loan won't take long, did it?* (ad.: savings and loan)

20. *What did you bring that book I don't want to be read to out of up for?* (syndicated column, newspaper)

21. *Name another large country besides Holland.* (overheard)

22. *The nonstop nonstop airline to Houston.* (ad.)

23. *What you don't know about painting would fill a book ... and* [paint brand] *wrote it.* (ad.: house paint)

24. *Brazil. In ten years, they'll talk about the way it was now.* (ad.: airline)

25. *Colorless green ideas sleep furiously.* (N. Chomsky 1957)

ASSIGNMENT G* **Grammatical Relations**

A change in grammatical relations in an English sentence can come about through use of the **passive** (e.g. *Mary loves John ~ John is loved by Mary*). Simply render into the passive each example below, turning on the *italicized* verb. Be sure not to change the meaning in any other way.

1. John Harvard *founded* Harvard University.
    Harvard University *was founded by John Harvard* . . . .

2. Most of us will *need* a lot of help.
    A lot of help . . . .

3. The Cubs might *win* the pennant by 1999.
    The pennant . . . .

4. Having to learn English *disturbs* a few people in the world.
    A few people in the world . . . .

5. The report said that the hurricane *killed* a lot of people.
    The report said that a . . . .

6. Who knows where you can *find* a good restaurant around here?
    Who knows where a . . . .

7. The weather bureau *predicted* that there would be rain.
    That there . . . .

8. A lot of people must have *lived* in this house.
    This house . . . .

9. Everybody failed to *notice* the crack in the foundation.
    The crack in the foundation . . . .

10. What can you *say* about it?
    What can . . . .

ASSIGNMENT **Ambiguity**
H*

The following examples of **telegraphese** (typically truncated captions) all have possible intrpretations that are different from those intended. That is, they are ambiguous. After examining them, indicate whether you think the ambiguity is traceable to constituency, grammatical relations, single lexical items, or possibly something else. All the examples are taken from a column appearing in the *Columbia Journalism Review*.

1. LIFE MEANS CARING FOR HOSPITAL DIRECTOR [Hamilton, Ont., *Spectator*]

2. DISMEMBERMENT KILLER CONVICTED / 'Thank God the jury could put the pieces together' [Brockton, MA, *Enterprise*]

3. LIFE SENTENCE STRETCHED BY CURSED JUDGE [N.O. *Times Picayune*]

4. DOWNTOWN HOGS GRANT CASH [Chicago *Tribune*]

5. U.S. APPROVES RIGHT TO VOTE FOR RELEASED TEXAS FELONS [Houston *Chronicle*]

6. 20,000 AT MASS FOR POLISH PRIEST REPORTED KILLED [*Stars & Stripes*]

7. LATE BUS COORDINATOR REMEMBERED [New London, CT, *Day*]

8. MAN MINUS EAR WAIVES HEARING [Jackson, TN, *Sun*]

9. HOW TO COMBAT THAT FEELING OF HELPLESSNESS WITH ILLEGAL DRUGS [Bermuda, *Royal Gazette*]

10. LARGE CHURCH PLANS COLLAPSE [Hamilton, Ont., *Spectator*]

11. HEMORRHOID VICTIM TURNS TO ICE [Milwaukee *Sentinel*]

12. OWNERS RESPONSIBLE FOR BITING CANINES (New Albany, IN, *Tribune*]

PART I

Grammatical Constructs and Configurations

SECTION A Grammatical Category: NP, DP

ASSIGNMENT 1* **The Noun Phrase**

The **noun phrase** (NP) can vary in length between a single word – e.g. *Mary* – and a string consisting of multiple sub-parts and indefinite length: *important decisions about whether or not to speak up that people have to make.* Both NPs contain a **head** – *Mary* and *decisions* – as do all NPs, and *decisions* in the second example happens to contain modifying material on either side of it. Good tests of whether or not a sequence of words constitutes an NP are to question it with a wh-word, *who* or *what,* or to substitute a pronoun for it. Thus:

Here's *Mary*   / Here *she* is

Here are *some of the many important decisions about whether or not to speak up that people have to make* / Here *they* are

In each of the following sentences, underline the FULL NP whose head is *italicized.*

1.   The army wants the *women* for special training.

2.   Nobody will know the *answer* to a question like that, I bet.

3.   If you think that problem's hard, wait till you see the *one* on the home-work we have to hand in tomorrow.

4.   We happened to see the *accident* on the way home from the beach.

5.   Last night a TV *program* about wild animals came on too late for us to watch.

6.   Where does it say that *immigrants* have to swear an allegiance to the state?

7.   So you're looking for a *book* about linguistics that can serve as an intro-ductory text in a course for advanced undergraduates.

8.   Great *oaks* from little acorns grow.

9.   Don't forget to put the *books* on the shelf.

10.   Don't forget to put the *books* on the shelf back where they belong.

ASSIGNMENT 2* Nouns and Determiners

It has been noted that the **singular/plural** distinction for nouns in English is far from adequate for rendering an accounting of what determiners may co-occur with what nouns. Huddleston (1984: 245) notes that "inherently plural *surroundings* cannot combine with *every* nor inherently singular *phonetics* with *many*." Note in addition the ungrammaticality of examples like **two clothes*, **another equipment*, etc. We thus need to conceive of nouns in terms of degree of **countability**. Again, in the words of Huddleston (1984: 245),

> at one extreme we have uncountable nouns like *equipment*, which are incompatible with any of the following determiners:
>
> (a)   the cardinal numerals *one, two, three*, etc.
>
> (b)   other numerically quantifying expressions such as *both, a dozen*, etc.
>
> (c)   the "fuzzy" quantifiers *many, several, few*;
>
> (d)   *a, another, each, every, either, neither*, which take singular heads.
>
> At the other extreme we have fully countable nouns like *dog*, which can combine with any of these (given the appropriate number inflection, of course).

Furthermore, it is possible to interpret **count** nouns as **non-count** when what is at issue is the "substance" and not the discrete entity – e.g. *a lot of cake* vs. *a lot of cakes*.

With reference to these distinctions, construct a continuum of countability in this way: Group the nouns listed below in terms of the above determiners (a–d) with which the nouns can co-occur and range them on a scale of "uncountable" to "fully countable." Add other nouns of your own to the classification.

> *cake, police, vocabulary, knowledge, cattle, people, outskirts,*
> *word, dregs, air, clothes, happiness*

(continued)

Name: _____   Date: __ / __ / __   Class: _____

Examples   Determiners permitted from list

Uncountable:

Fully countable:

ASSIGNMENT 3* **Definiteness**

Deployment of the **definite article** in English is invoked in a range of contexts that goes considerably beyond any simple notion of "definiteness." The major instances of such deployment are something like the following:

(a) inherently **unique** common nouns:
      *the earth, **the** moon, **the** sky*, etc.

(b) **visible** to speaker and/or hearer:
      *the door, **the** window, **the** tree, **the** wall*, etc.

(c) generally **expected** or assumed to be present:
      *the police station, **the** post office, **the** market*, etc.

(d) **prior mention:** *(I bought **a** new house)*
      *It/**The** house has seven rooms / **The** place is terrific*

(e) **associative anaphora** (parts, attributes): *(I bought **a** new house)*
      *The kitchen is rather large / **The** price was high*

(f) **inherent property:**
      the jovial and witty Henry Kissinger
   cf. *a sullen and snappish Henry Kissinger*
      (*a/*the) Henry Kissinger

(g) referent-establishing **relative clause:**
      I talked with the (one/only/last) student who needed help
   cf. *?I talked with the (one/only/last) student*

(h) referent-establishing **noun complement:**
      the fact that the world is round
      the need to eliminate guns
      the decision to leave/ . . . that we should leave

(i) **apposition:**
      The/*a color blue is my favorite
      I can't stand the/*a name "Fafnir"
      Take a chance on the/*a number seven

(j) **genericness:**
      The lizard is a reptile

(continued)

31

Name: _____ Date: __ / __ / __ Class: _____

For each instance of *the* in the sentences below, indicate one (or more) of the following:

unique (U)	prior mention (PM)	referent-establishing RC (RC)
visible (V)	associative anaphora (AA)	referent-establishing NC (NC)
expected (E)	inherent property (IP)	apposition (A)
		generic (G)

Are there any *the*s below not accounted for in this list?

1. . . . . . They had to take him to *the* hospital

2. . . . . . Stone was *the* first material to be used for tools

3. . . . . . When you have a wedding *the* bride is given away

4. . . . . . *The* sabre-tooth tiger once inhabited North America

5. . . . . . There was a wedding, and *the* nuptials made the front page

6. . . . . . There she is – *the* always smiling Mrs Springfield

7. . . . . . Can you reach *the* top shelf?

8. . . . . . Does *the* name "Zumberg" mean anything to you?

9. . . . . . We find *the* defendant "not guilty"

10. . . . . . I don't buy *the* verdict that he's guilty

11. . . . . . Have a seat out in *the* waiting room

12. . . . . . I know you need it, but where you gonna get *the* funds?

13. . . . . . What do you buy for *the* woman who has everything?

14. . . . . . Try to control *the* urge to say something

15. . . . . . Universal Grammar must have something to do with *the* universe

16. . . . . . *The* place to look for it is the Yellow Pages

17. . . . . . Don't tell me I'm standing here talking to THE Ollie North!

18. . . . . . Beware of *the* dog!

19. . . . . . Have you ever seen *the* film *Sunset Boulevard*?

20. . . . . . I was driving home yesterday when *the* fuel pump gave out

ASSIGNMENT 4* The Determiner Phrase

Traditional grammar books call phrases like *the book about linguistics, the important decisions, that car of his*, etc., **noun phrases**, as exemplified in Assignment 1. In more recent work, however, the head of a phrase like *the book about linguistics* is taken to be not the noun *book* but the determiner *the*. The whole construction is therefore a **determiner phrase** or **DP**, in which *book about linguistics* is an NP occurring as complement to the (head) determiner *the*. Older (NP) and newer (DP) representations of *the book about linguistics* in tree form would thus look like the following:

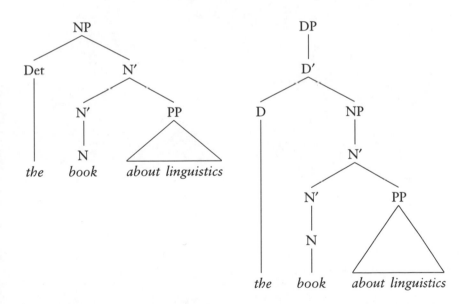

Some of the motivation for the DP/NP distinction will be seen in Assignment 8. The rationale for the intermediate N′/D′ level of structure will be seen in Assignment 7.

(continued)

For each of the following sentences, some of which are taken from Assignment 1, underline whatever words appear to you to be **determiners** – i.e. heads of DPs:

1. *The army wants good women for special training.*

2. *I'm looking for the answer to a certain question.*

3. *This is the right place.*

4. *If you think that problem's hard, wait till you see the one on the homework we have to hand in tomorrow.*

5. *Those books are on sale; these are not.*

6. *Great oaks from little acorns grow.*

7. *That's really a problem for us all.*

8. *Where does it say that immigrants have to swear allegiance to the state?*

ASSIGNMENT **Determiner**
5*   **System: L1**

One of the classic studies of child L1 acquisition is that of L. Bloom (1970). Lifted from this piece of research (pp. 41, 42) below is a representative sample from all of Bloom's data for two- and three-word utterances containing *this* and *thats* produced by one of her subjects (Kathryn) at the age of 21 months:

Description of speech event [M = mother; L = Lois, K's sister]		Kathryn's utterance
Let's go find a book to read.		
(K picking up a book about babies)	(a)	*this* baby book
(M putting slipper on K)	(b)	*this* slipper
(M trimming L's fingernails)	(c)	*this* hand now
(K picking up dirty sock)	(d)	*this* dirty
(K standing at balcony door; looking out at cold winter day)	(e)	*thats* cold

Radford (1990) offers the following examples of the occurrence of *this* and *that* in utterances of one of his subjects (Daniel) at the age of 19–21 months (the adult equivalents are supplied by Radford):

(f)   *That* chair (= "That is a chair")
(g)   Want *that*
(h)   *That* daddy there (= "That's daddy there")
(i)   *That* doggy (= "That's a doggy")
(j)   *This* tree (= "This is a tree")
(k)   Want *this*
(l)   What's *that*
(m)   *That*'s bee

(continued)

Radford (1990) argues on the basis of these and other, related data that the child's early grammar is characterized by the absence of a determiner system. In what way can Radford's data be used to support that argument? Briefly, how would Kathryn's utterances in Bloom's data need to be interpreted if they also are to be construed as support for Radford's argument? Which of Bloom's examples would prove problematic for that argument? (Consider that the child may have acquired a lexical item identifiable as a determiner but without analyzing it as the head of a DP.)

Name: _____   Date: __ / __ / __   Class: _____

ASSIGNMENT 6*   Phrasal Categories: NP (I)

Formal linguistics commonly distinguishes between **complements** and **adjuncts**. These can be represented within the NP by the kind of prepositional phrase (PP) that may follow the head noun. For example, the PP following the noun *teacher* in *a teacher of linguistics* is a **complement**; that following *teacher* in *a teacher from Harvard* is an **adjunct**. Listed below are some criteria for drawing these distinctions; each is sufficient, though not all are necessary.

- **ordering** (complement before adjunct):
  a teacher *of linguistics from Harvard* / ?a teacher *from Harvard of linguistics*

- **wh-question** (only of complements):
  What is she a teacher *of*? / *What* is she a teacher *from*?

- **pro-N'** (only of adjuncts; see Assignment 88):
  the *one from Harvard* / ?the *one of linguistics*

- **stacking** (only of adjuncts):
  a teacher *from Harvard from England*
  *a teacher *of linguistics of history*

- **co-occurrence** (limited of complements):
  a teacher/student/*girl/*letter/*offer/*degree/etc. *of linguistics*
  a teacher/student/girl/letter/offer/degree/etc. *from Harvard*

(continued)

For the NPs [bracketed] in each of the following pairs, mark "A" if it contains an adjunct, "C" if it contains a complement, and both if it is ambiguous. Adjuncts and complements are *italicized*.

1. ····· the [article *on desks*]

2. ····· the [article *on the desk*]

3. ····· a [constant search *for knowledge*]

4. ····· a [constant search *for nothing*]

5. ····· [interest *in an affair*]

6. ····· [interest *in an account*]

7. ····· [imprisonment *for a year*]

8. ····· [imprisonment *for theft*]

9. ····· a [mad dash *after the bus*]

10. ····· a [mad dash *after the bus's arrival*]

11. ····· [arrival *at the station*]

12. ····· [arrival *at six*]

13. ····· a [ruler *of no consequence*]

14. ····· a [ruler *of no country*]

15. ····· [pain *over his failure*]

16. ····· [pain *over his face*]

17. ····· a [garden *of floral beauty*]

18. ····· a [garden *of beautiful flowers*]

19. ····· [success *in other institutions*]

20. ····· [success *in passing courses*]

Name: _____   Date: __ / __ / __   Class: _____

Phrasal Categories: NP (II)

The standard convention for basic phrase-structure representation can be seen as a "template" accommodating all the lexical categories: noun, verb, adjective, preposition. Letting "X" stand for any of these categories, the template will look like this, where X is the **head** and XP its **maximal projection** and where the parenthesized **specifier** and **complement** are made use of when needed (see below):

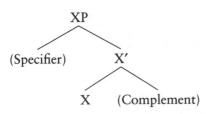

The PS representation of a word like *teacher* would therefore quite simply be:

teacher

The intermediate level represented as X' (read "X-bar") lends its name to phrase-structure syntax as a whole, termed **X-bar syntax**.

Noun modifiers like adjective (phrases) and prepositional phrases are **adjuncts** in X-bar terms and enter the X-bar configuration via **adjunction to X'**. Adjunction then results in the copying or creation of another X' node, as in either of the following:

(continued)

39

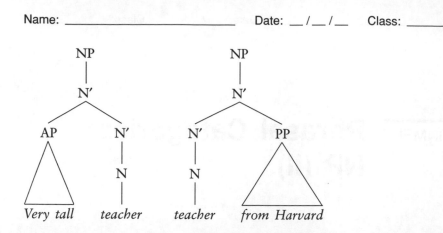

Very tall   teacher   teacher   from Harvard

The formal distinction between a **complement** (e.g. *of history*) and an **adjunct** (e.g. *from Harvard*) of a head noun (e.g. *teacher*) can therefore be represented in terms of an X-bar schema like the following, in which the complement is sister of N and the adjunct is sister of N-bar:

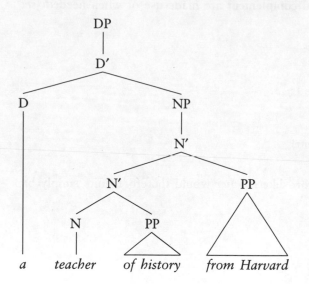

a   teacher   of history   from Harvard

Draw appropriate trees for the following noun phrases in the manner exemplified above, where the prepositional phrases are for now left unanalyzed:

1. *a king of England*
2. *a king from Germany*
3. *a king of England from Germany*
4. *a garden of beautiful flowers*
5. *a garden of floral beauty*
6. *arrival by ship by six*

(continued)

ASSIGNMENT 8** DP and NP

We saw in Assignment 4 that a phrase like *the book about linguistics* is a DP with *the* as head (D) and *book about linguistics* as its NP complement. It turns out that DP is needed for more than just the repository of definite articles and demonstratives like *this/that/these/those*. The DP houses **personal pronouns, possessives,** and **case agreement features** as well. That is, whereas *the* in *the queen* occurs as head of its DP, the possessive *her* in the DP *her majesty* occupies the **specifier** position of that DP, where *her* heads its own DP projection (i.e. DP₂) and the head of the higher DP (i.e. DP₁) contains the possessive agreement features:

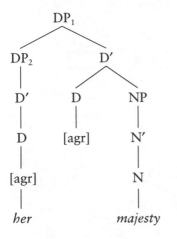

Accordingly, the analysis of a DP like *the queen's majesty* will be one in which the DP *the queen* occurs as specifier of the DP headed by the genitive inflection *'s*.

One additional fact of English to be captured by the DP/NP distinction has to do with possible ambiguity associated with use of the **indefinite article** *a(n)*. Consider a sentence like *I'm looking for a pin*. The "pin" in question might be a **specific** one – for example, one that I have momentarily misplaced. Or it might be **non-specific** – that is, just a pin for holding something in place; any pin will do. Pronominal replacements for these two senses of *a pin* will serve to highlight the contrast. An appropriate follow-up to *I'm looking for a* [specific] *pin* could be *Can you help me find it*, whereas the follow-up to non-specific *a pin* could be *Can you help me find one*. It has been proposed that the **specific** indefinites
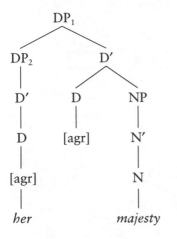(continued)

Name: _____   Date: __ / __ / __   Class: _____

be analyzed as DPs and the **non-specific** as NPs. In the latter, the determiner *a(n)* will simply be *inserted* in Spec, NP.

In the four trees below, enter both the category labels and the lexicon for the following phrases:

a [certain] *light blue pencil*
a light blue pencil [of any kind]
his light blue pencil
the boy in the back of the room's light blue pencil

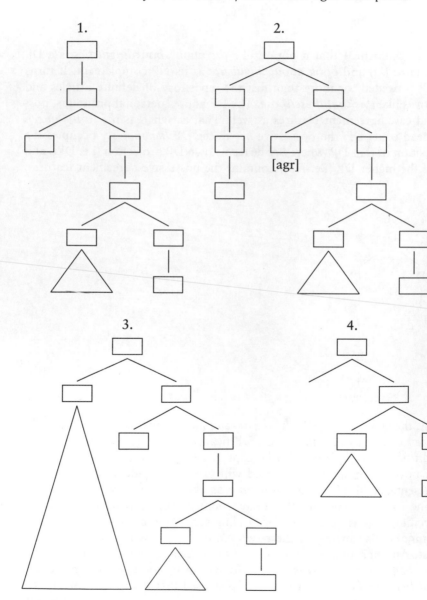

ASSIGNMENT 9* DP and NP: L1

Recall from Assignment 5 the argument that children's early grammars lack a determiner system or DP. The following data, culled from a classic research study of more than three decades ago (Brown and Bellugi 1964), are representative of utterances produced by two children between the ages of two and three:

(a) *a blue flower*
(b) *a nice nap*
(c) *a my pencil*
(d) *a your car*
(e) *a this truck*

Briefly, how might examples like these be interpreted to support a claim that early grammars are devoid of a determiner system?

Recall from the previous assignment the classification of indefinite NPs as specific and non-specific. It is generally believed that children are conservative in the development of their grammars; that is, they will expand their grammatical systems as the need arises and as they become aware of positive evidence for doing so. How then might the above examples support the notion of conservatism in the child's acquisition of a fully developed DP?

ASSIGNMENT 10* Code-Switching and the Structure of NP

(data from Woolford 1983)

Fluent bilingual speakers often produce sentences that are a mixture of their two languages, a practice referred to as **code-switching**. Not just ANY combination of the two languages is permissible, however; some combinations are perceived as "ungrammatical." Consider the following Spanish/English code-switching data, where the starred examples are considered not acceptable by most fluent code-switchers of these two languages. The full Spanish DPs are provided in brackets:

1. *The hombre viejo is mad*   [el hombre viejo]
   "The old man . . ."

2. *El old man está enojado*
   "The old man . . ."

3. *the white casa*   [la casa blanca]
   "the white house"

4. *el siguiente play*   [el siguiente juego]
   "the following play"

5. *the big casa*   [la gran casa]
   "the big house"

6. **the casa big*   [la casa grande]
   "the big house"

7. *this little abastos*   [este abastos chiquito]
   "this little grocery store"

8. **this abastos little*
   "this little grocery store"

9. **I went to the house chiquita*   [la casa chiquita]
   ". . . the little house"

(continued)

10.   *El man viejo está enojado*   [el hombre viejo]
       "The old man ..."

11.   *El hombre old está enojado*
       "The old man ..."

     See if you can determine how this pattern of code-switching data follows from the internal structure of noun phrases, where the noun and its adjective modifiers form a constituent separate from the determiner. Specifically, what accounts for the ungrammaticality of the starred examples? It will be helpful to observe that Spanish allows some adjectives to PRECEDE the noun, as shown in the full Spanish versions of nos. 4 and 5.

SECTION B Grammatical Category: VP, AP, PP, IP, CP

ASSIGNMENT 11* Arguments of the Verb

For each of the verbs listed below, first cite the number of arguments (i.e. referring expressions) it selects, if any. Ignore for now the distinction between internal (i.e. within the VP) and external (i.e. subject). (This is equivalent to traditional classification in terms of a "one-/two-/three-place predicate.") Then provide a sample sentence with the arguments exemplified. Note, however, that not all arguments of any given verb are necessarily obligatory. Note also that an argument may consist of **clausal** material – e.g. *Mary thinks She's smart.*

		No.	Example
1.	*walk*	1	*We walked*
2.	*hit*	2	*Mary hit John*
3.	*collapse*		
4.	*give*		
5.	*rain*		
6.	*put*		
7.	*die*		
8.	*blame*		
9.	*see*		
10.	*regret*		
11.	*doze*		
12.	*happen*		
13.	*push*		
14.	*supply*		
15.	*appear*		
16.	*fear*		

Name: _____   Date: __ / __ / __   Class: _____

ASSIGNMENT 12* Phrasal Categories: VP

We have already seen (Assignment 7) that all phrasal categories (XP) are analyzable in terms of the components **specifier, head, complement,** and **adjunct.** Here we will be concerned with the VP, its head, and any complement and adjunct that may occur with it. (There is a rough correspondence between the traditional notion **argument** – cf. the previous assignment – and more formal **complement:** All complements are arguments, though not necessarily vice versa.) The V that occurs as head of VP is the **lexical** verb, thereby excluding **auxiliaries** (forms of *do, be, have*), **modals** (*can, will, may*, etc.), and the inflectional elements (*-ed, -s*), none of which are properly part of the VP (cf. Assignment 14). By way of illustration, the separated VP portion of the first sentence from Assignment 4 would look like this:

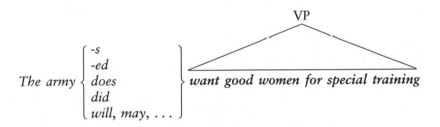

$$
\text{The army} \left\{ \begin{array}{l} \text{-s} \\ \text{-ed} \\ \text{does} \\ \text{did} \\ \text{will, may, } \ldots \end{array} \right\}
$$

Put brackets around the VP in each of the sentences below and underline and label its internal components as identified above. For the purpose of this assignment, use "H" for head, and (if they appear) "C" for complement and "A" for adjunct. Keep in mind that these are not grammatical categories but rather terms denoting grammatical function.

For example:

Does he [*live in London*?]
      H   *C*

1. *They will look at the results.*

2. *Who did insist on their coming on time?*

3. *Does anyone strongly insist on their coming on this report?*

(continued)

51

4. *The candidates didn't lay their cards on the table.*

5. *The hens didn't lay their eggs in the chicken coop.*

6. *Must they always rail against the authorities in power?*

7. *Blame all your troubles on the government all your life, will you?*

8. *Did she sort of blow up about being asked?*

9. *Why do you act so surprised at her reaction.*

10. *We'll keep our lunch in the refrigerator but eat it in the park.*

ASSIGNMENT 13* **Phrasal Categories: VP, AP, PP**

As was first seen in Assignment 7, adjectives and adverbs are **adjuncts** in X-bar terms and enter the X-bar configuration via **adjunction** to X′:

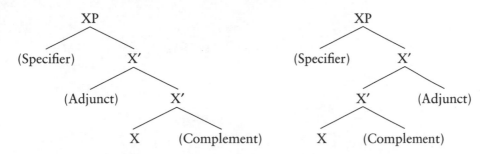

Although branching in these configurations is represented here as **binary**, there are those who argue for **ternary** branching in the case of phrasal heads analyzed as taking TWO complements. An example would be the VP *put the book on the shelf*:

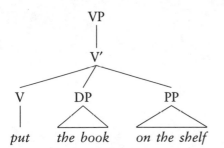

For this and a number of subsequent assignments in Part I, we will assume a representation for a head + two complements in which both complements are sisters to the head, as in the above.

Draw trees for the bracketed constituents in each of the examples below and represent these constituents as X-bar formulations in accord with the above conventions. For the purposes of this exercise, represent *to know what to do* in no. 3 as an unanalyzed CP (see the next assignment); represent *very* (no. 2) and

(continued)

somewhat (no. 3) as a special variety of adverb termed **intensifier** and occupying the specifier position.

1. They can [easily blame the accident on the police]

2. It looks [very similar to theirs in shape]

3. He's [somewhat at a loss to know what to do]

<hr>

ASSIGNMENT **Phrasal Categories:**
14* **IP, CP**

We have seen so far that VP, DP, NP, AP, and PP are (maximal) phrasal projections of their lexical heads: V(erb), D(eterminer), N(oun), A(djective), and P(reposition). There are other phrasal categories needed in grammatical analysis of the sentence itself. Two of these (with a somewhat simplified description here) would be, for example:

- IP or **INFL phrase**, exemplified by those portions of the following in **bold face**, where *I* (the head) is in *italics*:
  We believe that **he *must* be very patient**
  We believe   **him *to* be very patient**

The simplified representation in tree form would look like this:

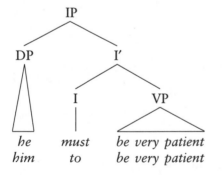

- CP or **complement phrase**, containing an IP preceded by a complementizer, exemplified by those portions of the following in *italics*, where C (the head) is in **bold face:**
  We believe   ***(that)** he must be very patient*
  We asked   ***for** him to be very patient*
  We doubted ***if** he was very patient*

(continued)

The simplified representation in tree form would look like this:

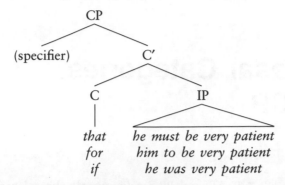

The *italicized* constituent(s) in the sentences below represent one or another of the phrasal categories VP, DP, AP, PP, CP, IP. Identify the category of each such constituent.

1. We look forward to taking a trip *to Alaska*   . . . . .

2. We look forward to taking *a trip to Alaska*   . . . . .

3. We look forward to *taking a trip to Alaska*   . . . . .

4. We look forward *to taking a trip to Alaska*   . . . . .

5. Is it possible *for you to take a trip to Alaska*?   . . . . .

6. I've never known *you to lie*   . . . . .

7. If *I lied*, would you tell anyone?   . . . . .

8. *For him to lie* would be easy   . . . . .

9. For him to listen *to lies* would be easy   . . . . .

10. Notice *their eagerness for us to lie for him*   . . . . .

11. They're *eager for us to lie for him*   . . . . .

12. What they're doing is *always telling lies*   . . . . .

13. *Whether or not she tells lies* is the question   . . . . .

14. Did you ask *for her to be promoted*?   . . . . .

15. Did you ask *for her promotion*?   . . . . .

16. I'm *anxious that she be promoted*   . . . . .

17. I've been happy *ever since her promotion*   . . . . .

18. I've been happy *ever since she was promoted*   . . . . .

Phrasal Categories: IP and Agreement

IP or INFL phrase corresponds roughly to the **predicate** in more traditional terms. IP thus embraces both the inflectional portion and the VP portion of the predicate, the inflectional (together with the modals, infinitival *to*, and tense-carrier *do*) constituting the **head**. Contained within the inflectional portion then would be the features of verb tense (present or past), of person (1st, 2nd, 3rd), and of number (singular, plural). The subject and verb of the sentence must **agree** with respect to these features. (Although in more recent versions of the theory, tense and agreement themselves are elevated to phrasal-category status, we will continue to subsume these under INFL.)

Verb inflection in English is very impoverished, owing to well-known developments in the history of the language, and this can give rise to an occasional curiosity. English requires that subject–verb agreement be morphologically marked only for the 3rd-person singular, present tense, as in

MSG spoils the broth

And there is no overt marking for 3rd-person PLURAL, as in

MSG and sodium chloride spoilØ the broth

Why then do we say "spoils" instead of "spoil" in the well-known old saying,

Too many cooks spoils the broth

where the verb, in other words, is marked for 3rd-person SINGULAR?
Since it IS also possible to say, and with a different meaning,

Too many cooks spoil the broth

we therefore have two grammatical sentences that differ only in that the verb in one agrees with a subject that would be 3rd-person SINGULAR, the verb in the other with a subject that would be 3rd-person PLURAL. But the FORM of the subject is the same in both cases! How is this possible? What is going on?

Name: _____ Date: __ / __ / __ Class: _____

ASSIGNMENT # Phrasal Categories:
16**   # Small Clause

Presented in Assignment 14 were the analyses of two clausal categories. One was **IP**, or **INFL phrase**, representing the basic clause, or sentence. The other was **CP**, or **complementizer phrase**, the "shell," so to speak, within which the basic clause is situated. The CP contains both a C (the head) and an IP. The IP contains no C but of course I (the head). There is a third clausal category to be introduced here that is devoid of BOTH complementizer and INFL and aptly labeled **small clause**. The small clause comes in four varieties:

Verbal small clause: *I saw*   [*him **leave home***]
Nominal small clause: *I made*   [*him **an enemy***]
Prepositional small clause: *I want*   [*him **in school***]
Adjectival small clause: *I consider* [*him **apt to fail***]

Notice that the defining characteristic for each of the four bracketed sub-types above is that portion in bold type – namely, the VP *leave home*, the DP *an enemy*, the PP *in school*, and the AP *apt to fail*.

It has been proposed that each ENTIRE CLAUSE take on this phrasal designation, where the phrase's **specifier** position will be occupied by the DP-subject of the clause: *him* in the above examples. The possibilities for small-clause configuration can therefore be taken from the following:

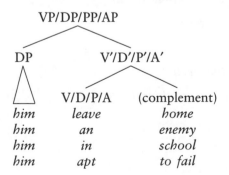

VP/DP/PP/AP

DP   V′/D′/P′/A′

      V/D/P/A   (complement)
him   *leave*   *home*
him   *an*   *enemy*
him   *in*   *school*
him   *apt*   *to fail*

Each of the four small-clause types illustrated above occurred as complement to a verb – namely, *see*, *make*, *want*, and *consider*, respectively. Verbs (as well

(continued)

as the other major lexical categories) that take complements are said to **sub-categorize** such complements, where **subcategorization** information includes not just the fact of complement-taking but also what TYPE of complement. Just as with *see*, *make*, *want*, and *consider*, the main verb in each of the examples below also subcategorizes a small clause, though none of the verbs except *have* subcategorizes all four small-clause types. That is, most of the verbs can occur with only a subset of the four types: adjectival (AP), prepositional (PP), nominal (DP), and verbal (VP). For each of the following sentences, underline the small clause and identify it according to type. Note that in nos. 4, 8, 11, and 13 the small clause occurs as complement to a verb in the passive, resulting in separation of the small-clause subject and predicate.

For example:

> We had <u>him come early</u>   *VP*

1. We consider him qualified for the job   . . . . .
2. I'll have you know that I travel a lot   . . . . .
3. Can you picture her in that dress?   . . . . .
4. "Notice Neptune, though, / Taming a sea-horse, thought a rarity" (Browning)   . . . . .
5. Did you find Sue as competent as Sally?   . . . . .
6. He says God made him do it   . . . . .
7. The bankruptcy left them paupers   . . . . .
8. Hondas are certainly rated above Fords   . . . . .
9. I now pronounce you man and wife   . . . . .
10. Did you see the man hit that little child!   . . . . .
11. Here you're assumed to be innocent until proven guilty   . . . . .
12. Imagine yourself on a desert island with nothing to eat   . . . . .
13. They're not exactly held in very high esteem   . . . . .
14. I hereby declare this person dead   . . . . .
15. They took him prisoner but treated him well   . . . . .
16. Watch them get mad when you do the same thing to THEM   . . . . .

ASSIGNMENT 17** Phrasal Categories: L1

In his book on L1 acquisition of English syntax, Radford (1990: ch. 6) cites many examples of utterances of a similar kind produced by children around the age of 18 to 24 months. These are examples such as the following:

A. *Hayley read that*   *Wayne not eating it*
    Mummy put it away   *Kathryn no like celery*
    Horse tumble   *Tina not have it*
    Her going on walk   *Man no go in there*
    Daddy sleeping

    That broken
    Car gone
    Lisa naughty

    Truck outside
    Shoes on
    Stephen in school

It is possible to draw an analogy between children's utterances like these and the virtually identical italicized portions of adult sentences like the following:

B. I made *Hayley read that*
    I can imagine *her going on a walk*
    I found *that broken*
    I had *Stephen in school*
    I saw *Wayne not eating it*

Radford in fact analyzes the child utterances in A as the SAME construction as that in the italicized portions of the sentences in B. What is the construction in question and what are its salient characteristics?

ASSIGNMENT 18* Grammatical Features

We have identified the four major lexical categories as **noun** (N), **verb** (V), **adjective** (A), and **preposition** (P). Among the world's languages, however, it is generally believed that only for nouns and verbs can arguments of any kind of universality be made; many languages lack the categories of adjective and/or preposition (more properly, **adposition**). Although nouns and verbs can therefore be considered more "basic," they themselves may be viewed as having complexes of features that constitute the building blocks for all four lexical categories. Those features are [±N] and [±V]. Accordingly, these four lexical categories can be identified in feature terms as follows:

noun: [+N, −V]
verb: [−N, +V]
adjective: [+N, +V]
preposition: [−N, −V]

Observe then that any one feature will serve to capture two of the above categories. [+N] alone, for example, singles out nouns and adjectives. Whenever two (or more) categories can together be distinguished with fewer features than either one of them singly, those categories are said to comprise a **natural class**. Representation of the lexical categories by means of the above features therefore implies the existence of four natural classes: namely, [+N], [−N], [+V], [−V]. Some of the possible justifications for positing their existence can be seen below.

Examine the following sets of (limited) language data, specify in feature terms the lexical categories at issue, and enter one of the four features [± V/N] to identify the corresponding natural class:

(continued)

Name: _____ Date: __ / __ / __ Class: _____

DATA	FEATURES	NATURAL CLASS

1.   *It interests me*
       It's interesting to me
    *It's very interesting me
    *It has a lot of interest me
	[,] and [,]
	assign objective case
		[ ]

2.   *seem* [*He to be tired*]
    He seems to be tired
    be likely [*He to be tired*]
    He is likely to be tired
	[,] and [,]
	license raising of subject
	in complement clause
	(see Assignment 67)
		[ ]

3.   *la mesa negra* (Spanish)
    la table noire (French)
    la tavola nera (Italian)
    "the black table"
	[,] and [,]
	show gender agreement
	in many languages
		[ ]

4.   (*Mary jogs in the morning*)
    It's in the morning that Mary jogs
    It's Mary who jogs in the morning
    *It's jog in the morning that Mary does
	[,] and [,]
	appear in **cleft sentence**
	or **focus** constructions
	(see Assignment 34)
		[ ]

Grammatical Features: Category and Subcategory (I)

What complements can the four major lexical categories (N, V, A, P) sub-categorize, given at least the theoretical possibility of NP, AP, VP, PP, in addition to Ø, CP, IP, and XP (the cover term here for small clause)? Write the example after the category for each possibility, some of which are already suggested. Finally, are there any regularities to be noted in the completed patterns?

N [+N, −V]

1. [NP]
2. [AP]
3. [VP]
4. [PP] *belief in hard work*
5. [Ø]
6. [CP]
7. [IP]
8. [XP]

V [−N, +V]

9. [NP]
10. [AP] *turn green*
11. [VP]
12. [PP]
13. [Ø]
14. [CP]
15. [IP]
16. [XP]

A [+N, +V]

17. [NP]
18. [AP]
19. [VP]
20. [PP]
21. [Ø]
22. [CP] *anxious that they behave*
23. [IP]
24. [XP]

P [−N, −V]

25. [NP]
26. [AP]
27. [VP]
28. [PP]
29. [Ø]
30. [CP]
31. [IP] *since the party began*
32. [XP]

Grammatical Features: Category and Subcategory (II)

ASSIGNMENT 20*

For each of the italicized lexical items below, identify both its categorial features – i.e. [± V/N] – and its subcategorization features – i.e. DP, PP, AP, IP, CP, XP [= small clause] – if any.

For example:

		CATEGORY	SUBCATEGORY
	I *made* a sandwich for her	[+V, −N]	[NP, PP]
1.	*Watch* the man on the trapeze	[,]	[
2.	*Watch* the man on the trapeze do a somersault	[,]	[
3.	a *need* for somebody to do something quickly	[,]	[
4.	*because* there's nothing to be done about it	[,]	[
5.	*because* of the fact that there's nothing to be done about it	[,]	[
6.	*prone* to getting a divorce every three years	[,]	[
7.	She *cut* her hair shorter than usual	[,]	[
8.	We have a problem *in* that we seem to be boxed in	[,]	[
9.	*Put* another record on	[,]	[
10.	*blame* for the accident on the police	[−V, +N]	[
11.	*Give* Mary something for Christmas	[,]	[
12.	*See* that the door is locked	[,]	[
13.	*See* to it right away	[,]	[
14.	See *to* it right away that the door is locked	[,]	[

ASSIGNMENT 21** Verb Subcategorization

Consider the following sentence frame and the three verbs – *believe, want, persuade* – chosen to fill it:

We *believed/wanted/persuaded* him to be more honest

Although it is tempting to think that all we have here is a single VP structure that can accommodate a variety of verbs, it will be helpful to verify this assumption. We can accomplish this by subjecting the infinitival portion of the VP to some familiar tests or diagnostics:

- **constituency** (i.e. whether *him to be more honest* is a constituent or not): yes for *believe* and *want*, no for *persuade*, as revealed in

- **paraphrasing with *that*-S:**
  We *believed/wanted/*persuaded* **that he should be more honest**

  or, conversely:
  We **believed/*wanted/persuaded* him **that he should be more honest**

- **insertion of the complementizer *for*** (perhaps not in all dialects):
  We **believed/wanted/*persuaded* **for him to be more honest**

  where the complementizer surfaces as well in

- **pseudo-clefting:**
  What we **believed/wanted/*persuaded* **was for him to be more honest**

On the basis of the results of these diagnostics, we can conclude that the three VPs headed by *believe, want, persuade* contain three distinct structures. Specifically:

> We *believed* [$_{IP}$ *him to be more honest*]
> We *wanted* [$_{CP}$ e [$_{IP}$ *him to be more honest*]]
> We *persuaded him* [$_{CP}$ e [$_{IP}$ PRO *to be more honest*]]

Therefore the *believe* class subcategorizes an IP complement; the *want* class subcategorizes a CP complement (with or without an overt complementizer),

(continued)

and the *persuade* class subcategorizes a DP as well as a CP complement. (For PRO, see Assignment 30.)

For each of the sentences listed, indicate whether the verb (*italicized*) subcategorizes one or two complements and whether the non-finite clausal complement is IP or CP.

For example:

We *believed* him to be more honest	.1.	. IP ..
We *wanted* him to be more honest	.1.	. CP ..
We *persuaded* him to be more honest	.2.	. CP ..

1. We *found* him to be more honest   ... .
2. We *expected* him to be more honest   ... .
3. We *discovered* him to be more honest   ... .
4. We *helped* him to be more honest   ... .
5. We *reminded* him to be more honest   ... .
6. We *considered* him to be more honest   ... .
7. We *taught* him to be more honest   ... .
8. We *imagined* him to be more honest   ... .
9. We *judged* him to be more honest   ... .
10. We *allowed* him to be more honest   ... .
11. We *liked* him to be more honest   ... .
12. We *urged* him to be more honest   ... .
13. We *asked* him to be more honest   ... .
14. We *told* him to be more honest   ... .
15. We *understood* him to be more honest   ... .
16. We *felt* him to be more honest   ... .
17. We *knew* him to be more honest   ... .
18. We *encouraged* him to be more honest   ... .
19. We *preferred* him to be more honest   ... .
20. We *invited* him to be more honest   ... .

ASSIGNMENT
22**

Complement vs. Adjunct: All Categories

With respect to the *italicized* constituent in each of the sentences below, mark "Ad" if you think it is an adjunct, "Cp" if a complement. Look to see if any of these could be both Ad AND Cp.

1. . . . . John urged Mary *to pay Max*

2. . . . . John robbed Mary *to pay Max*

3. . . . . They died *the following morning*

4. . . . . They wasted *the following morning*

5. . . . . She blew up *with his rudeness*

6. . . . . She put up *with his rudeness*

7. . . . . We decided *on the boat*

8. . . . . We decided *on the boat* on the plane

9. . . . . He should stop *to have lunch*

10. . . . . He should stop *having lunch*

11. . . . . A lot of people succeeded *in that town*

12. . . . . A lot of people succeeded *in moving to that town*

13. . . . . Put the letter *on the shelf*

14. . . . . Read the letter *on the shelf*

15. . . . . Read the letter *on your way home*

16. . . . . I helped him *to get ahead*

17. . . . . They're giving me a gift(,) *so I'll give them one*

18. . . . . Sally waved to Jim *to stop*

19. . . . . Sally waved to Jim$_i$ *to stop him$_i$*

20. . . . . The banks are trying to get more depositors *to increase their earnings*

ASSIGNMENT 23* Subcategorization: L2

The English learner-language examples listed below contain deviant forms (with respect to the target) that we will assume here are tied to subcategorization. For each of the *italicized* lexical items (and from the learner's perspective), identify both its categorial features – i.e. [± V/N] – and its subcategorization features – i.e. DP, PP, AP, IP, CP, XP [= small clause].

1. I *suggested* her to drive in a lot and hide

2. In present, to cover my faults, I am *devoted* to read textbooks and sidereaders

3. ... so I take calculus course. This is *useful* to solve many problems

4. I *avoid* to drink anything alcoholic

5. After the accident in which I involved I *make* a rule of my life that be slow and more careful at the time of crossing road

6. Thank you *for* you call me

ASSIGNMENT 24* VP **Structure**

The bracketed VPs in the examples below all have the superficial structure [V NP PP] but differ in their underlying structure, where at least a few of the examples are ambiguous. Identify the structure by number from the following list of five possibilities:

(a) V + small clause: *She **wanted** [me in the kitchen]*
(b) V + 2 complements (DP, PP):   *She **found** [a job] [for him]*
(c) V + complement + adjunct: *She **knew** [the answer] [in a second]*
(d) V + complement with modifier: *She **knew** [the answer to the question]*
(e) V + 2 complements (DP, small clause):   *She **quit** [the scene] [[PRO] in a huff]*

1. (   ) *Who thinks they [saw Max in the garage]*
2. (   ) *She finally [bought a gun to everyone's dismay]*
3. (   ) *He always [had his lunch in the refrigerator]*
4. (   ) *He always [had his lunch in the park]*
5. (   ) *He always [ate his lunch in a hurry]*
6. (   ) *Why don't you [write a letter to The Times]*
7. (   ) *Try to [get everybody in the photo]*
8. (   ) *Did you [notice anything out of place]*
9. (   ) *Did you [notice anything out of your window]*
10. (   ) *Did you [notice anything outside your window]*
11. (   ) *We should [call the assistant to the president]*
12. (   ) *We should [call the assistant to the phone]*
13. (   ) *We should [call the assistant on your phone]*
14. (   ) *I think you'll [find them in a quandary]*
15. (   ) *I think you'll [find them in a quarry]*
16. (   ) *Why did he [leave the room in tears]*
17. (   ) *Why did he [leave the room in tatters]*

ASSIGNMENT
25*

Phrasal Categories: CP, IP, DP, NP, VP, AP, PP

Provide the category labels and the lexicon for the tree (below) representing the structure of the following sentence:

The sentence on this page can represent one large constituent.

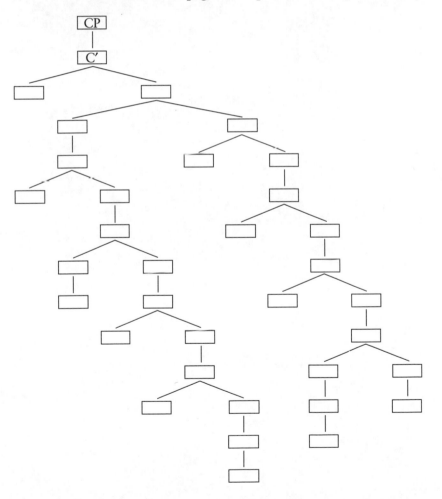

ASSIGNMENT 26** Coordination: L2

The following **interlanguage** (IL) examples are reproduced here with all learner errors unchanged. What is of interest for the purposes of this assignment, however, is the sentences containing instances of mismatched coordination. For each example, put brackets [ ] around the conjuncts in question and identify them by grammatical category.

For example:

Thank you for [the present] and [you help me]   *[NP] and [IP]*

1. *omitting a return address, forgetting to apply a postage stamp, putting a 13-cent stamp on letters requiring 26 cents, or the addressee refuses to pay postage due . . .*

   [   ], [   ], [   ], or [   ]

2. *The postman makes mistakes like these when he is nervous, angry, in a hurry, or something wrong with his relations with the post office.*

   [   ], [   ], [   ], or [   ]

3. *I think that he only wanted to say that Mexico not only has no advantages of being a neighbor of the US, but also disadvantages.*

   not only [   ], but also [   ]

4. *In my view Alaska pipeline is not going to be a solution to the US shortage of oil, because of many things such as high costs, earthquake, and it takes a long time . . .*

   [   ], [   ], and [   ]

5. *The law alows us to give this drugs to patients not only by one prescription like here but it must be taken by 3 prescriptions.*

   not only [   ] but [   ]

6. *The war'll damages everything in that areas. For example, the people was killed, the building was ruined, no school and have nothing except the war.*

   [   ], [   ], [   ], and [   ]

ASSIGNMENT 27** Phrasal Verbs

Consider the **bold type** portion of sentences in each of the following three groups:

A	B	C
*Look **up** the title*	*Look **at** the title*	*Look **up at** the title*
Look **up it*	*Look **at** it*	*Look **up at** it*
*Look the title **up***	**Look the title **at***	**Look the title **up at***
*Look it **up***	**Look it **at***	**Look it **up at***
Look now **up the title*	*Look now **at** the title*	**Look now **up at** the title*
*Look **up** *(the title)*	*Look **at** *(the title)*	*Look **up** (at the title)*
*It was **looked úp***	*It was **lóoked àt***	*?It was **looked up at***

Shown above are three verbs consisting of more than one word, often called **phrasal verbs**. The three represent three different types, however, as can readily be seen in their displayed characteristics. Perhaps the most salient of these are the following:

- *look up* in A is a **transitive verb-particle** construction whose direct object can separate the two and must do so if it is a pronoun; the constituency is *look up* + DP, and the verb-particle is a semantic unit.

- *look at* in B is a **verb-preposition** construction in which the preposition naturally heads a prepositional phrase occurring as complement to the verb; the constituency is *look* + PP, and the verb-preposition is therefore not a semantic unit.

- *look up* in C is an **intransitive verb-particle** construction; its constituency is simply *look up*, and the verb-particle is therefore a semantic unit.

(continued)

Mark the phrasal verbs in *italics* as "prt/t" for **verb-particle/transitive**, "prep" for **verb-preposition**, or "prt/i" for **verb-particle/intransitive**. Mark a construction Ø if it is none of these. In analyzing, make use of the above criteria – namely, constituency, separability, semantic wholeness, etc. Finally, what is unusual about the statement in no. 20?

1. *Look up* the title   ....*prt/t*....

2. *Look at* the title   ....*prep*....

3. *Look up at* the title   ....*prt/i*....

4. The eighteenth century *believed in* the scientific method   ....

5. The eighteenth century *brought in* the scientific method   ....

6. *Look out!*   ....

7. *Try on* that hat over there on the table   ....

8. Let's *move on* tomorrow   ....

9. *Plan on* that dinner over there in the evening   ....

10. Why don't you *leave out* tomorrow from your schedule?   ....

11. Why don't you *go out* tomorrow during the meeting?   ....

12. *Clean off* your shoes   ....

13. *Stay off* your feet   ....

14. *Off* we *go!*   ....

15. Go *away!*   ....

16. What did they *call for?*   ....

17. What did they call him for?   ....

18. We think we'll *take off* tomorrow   ....

19. What did you *bring* that book I don't want to be read to out of *up* for?   ....

20. "Ending a sentence with a preposition is something *up with* which I will not *put*" (Winston Churchill)   ....

ASSIGNMENT 28*   Phrasal Verbs: L1

One of the earliest inquiries into child language development in which phrasal-verb data were obtained is a study by Menyuk (1969). Menyuk's subjects were 152 children ranging in age from $3\frac{1}{2}$ to $4\frac{1}{2}$ and the data were elicited and tape recorded in several stimulus–response situations. Eighty-nine percent of the children produced verb-particle sequences in which **verb** and **particle** are separated by the direct object, as in *He put his clothes on* (cf. *He put on his clothes*). Recall from the previous assignment that separation is obligatory if the object is a pronoun:

He put them on / **He put on them*

Menyuk states that:

in some instances the children ... do not observe this restriction. They produce utterances [*italics* and **bold type** added] such as:

You pick up it
He took out her
Joanna took off them
He beat up him

These utterances occur ... most frequently with the pronoun "it." "Pick up," "put on," and "take off" are the most frequently used verb + particle forms found. (1969: 94)

Since the children presumably would have encountered in their input only the grammatical versions of these – i.e. where the pronoun separates verb and particle – what plausible explanation can you think of for why some of them might be producing the UNgrammatical sequences?

SECTION C C-Command and Control

Name: _____ Date: __ / __ / __ Class: _____

C-Command

Introduced in Assignment 8 was an analysis of DP that embraced possessives, demonstratives, personal pronouns, and case agreement features. The possessive example was the following:

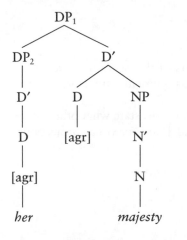

The fact that pronouns show case distinctions (*she, her*) has to be built in to the model if constructions like *she majesty* or *her reigned* are to be ruled out. This is accomplished by a "matching" of the case features within [agr] under the **head** of DP_1 – in this case, features of possessive – with the case features within [agr] under the **specifier** of DP_1 (i.e. DP_2), realized here by possessive *her*. The agreement thus achieved is termed **specifier–head** (or **Spec–head**) agreement, and it generalizes to other instances of a specifier–head relationship (e.g. subject–verb agreement).

A constant pattern is therefore to be noted with pairs of agreeing elements in a Spec–head relationship: Neither one dominates the other, one is always higher than the other, and some node (in fact a **maximal projection**) dominating the higher will also dominate the lower. This pattern of structural relations has been realized as a principle of **constituent command** or **c-command**. The standard statement of the principle is the following:

> X c-commands Y if and only if X does not dominate Y, nor Y dominate X, and the first maximal projection that dominates X also dominates Y.

(continued)

87

Name: _____   Date: __ / __ / __   Class: _____

This c-command statement and the X, Y, Z symbols can be illustrated by reference to the above possessive structure, as follows:

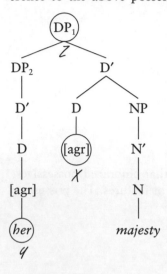

C-command will figure in the last three assignments of this section as well as in a number of later assignments concerning case assignment, movement, reference, etc.

For each node in the phrase structure configuation below, state what other nodes (if any!) it c-commands. Assume that A, B, D, and F are maximal projections.

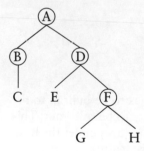

1. A c-commands . . . .

2. B c-commands . . . .

3. C c-commands . . . .

4. D c-commands . . . .

5. E c-commands . . . .

6. F c-commands . . . .

7. G c-commands . . . .

8. H c-commands . . . .

ASSIGNMENT 30** **Control and PRO**

It is generally assumed that a sentence like *John is thinking about* [$_{CP}$ *whether to buy himself a present*] is one in which the antecedent of the reflexive *himself* must be found within the bracketed CP. Since there is no overt NP antecedent, a covert one – namely, **PRO** – serves in its place. PRO in turn receives here its interpretation in relation to (and is coindexed with) the matrix subject, *John*, yielding the following:

John$_i$ is thinking about [$_{CP}$ *whether* [$_{IP}$ PRO$_i$ *to buy himself a present*]]

John, the matrix subject, is therefore said to **control** PRO, and in fact must c-command it. PRO then, an abstract syntactic element, always stands in for the missing overt NP subject of an infinitival clause and the coindexing of PRO with its NP antecedent allows the otherwise missing subject of the infinitive to be interpreted as that antecedent.

Represent each of the sentences below in bracketed notation and in the manner illustrated above. Deploy the bracketing only for the infinitival clause. Finally, comment on the relationship between no. 1 and no. 4.

1. *Jim told Max to drive*

2. *Max was told how to drive*

3. *Max was happy to drive*

4. *Jim promised Max to drive*

In bracketing the following, consider the status of coindexing and comment on the interpretation of PRO in such sentences.

5. *To err is human; to forgive (is) divine*

6. *The boat was sunk to collect the insurance*

Name: _____   Date: __ / __ / __   Class: _____

ASSIGNMENT 31* C-Command: L1

Experiments with young children to probe their understanding of referential relations have made use of sentences with internal structure like the following:

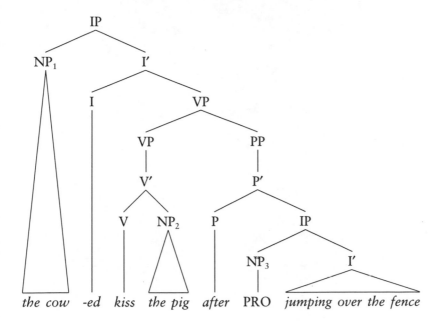

It has been noted that children often interpret the subject of *jumping* (i.e. NP$_3$ = PRO) as *the pig* rather than *the cow*; in other words, for these children *the pig* and not *the cow* is the **controller** of PRO. Children thus seem to have a control interpretation based upon the PROXIMITY of the controller to PRO, an invocation of what has sometimes been called the **Minimal Distance Principle** (**MDP**), formulated originally by C. Chomsky (1969).

Explain briefly how in this example the MDP runs afoul of the principle of c-command.

ASSIGNMENT
32**

Control and PRO: L1

The sizable quantity of research data on the development of child language comprehension and production that are analyzable in terms of PRO and control phenomena have suggested, depending on the age of the child (and on the data), that there may be more than one force at work in the child's language competence. Understanding of such constructions seems at times to show the force to be a **syntactic** one (i.e. c-command), a **semantic** one (i.e. identification of "agent": as the antecedent of PRO), or a **processing** one (i.e. minimal distance).

Listed below are examples of sentences figuring in one or another research study designed to test children's comprehension of control relations involving PRO, with the child's interpretation indicated via the analyst's coindexing of PRO and the antecedent chosen by the child. Indicate for each example which force the child's understanding might be based on by writing "s" (syntax), "m" (semantics), "p" (processing), or any combination of these.

1. *The cow kissed the pig$_i$ [after PRO$_i$ jumping over the fence]* (Foster 1990) . . . .

2. *John told Bill$_i$ [PRO$_i$ to grab the jewels]* (C. Chomsky 1969) . . . .

3. *John promised Bill$_i$ [PRO$_i$ to grab the jewels]* (C. Chomsky 1969) . . . .

4. *Fred$_i$ kissed Jane [before PRO$_i$ leaving]* (Goodluck 1991) . . . .

5. *Jane was kissed by Fred$_i$ [before PRO$_i$ leaving]* (Goodluck 1991) . . . .

6. *This doll$_i$ is hard [PRO$_i$ to see e]* (C. Chomsky 1969) . . . .

7. *Grover gives a sponge to Bert$_i$ [before PRO$_i$ falling into the water]* (McDaniel et al. 1990/1) . . . .

8. *John hit Bill$_i$ [PRO$_i$ carrying the basket]* (Goodluck 1981) . . . .

9. *John saw Bill$_i$ [PRO$_i$ carrying the basket]* (Goodluck 1981) . . . .

10. *Pluto$_i$ was chosen by Daisy [PRO$_i$ to do some reading]* (Goodluck and Behne 1992) . . . .

ASSIGNMENT 33*** Control and PRO: L2

Observed in the previous assignment is the fact that PRO works within a fixed domain, in that it will have a c-commanding antecedent (if any), and that young children learning their native English are apparently prone occasionally to letting something over-ride c-command – e.g. minimal distance. What then of PRO, control, c-command, and language learning in adulthood? A recent study (Martohardjono and Flynn 1995) looked at acquisition of English control structures by learners with three different native languages: Chinese, Japanese, and Spanish. The object of the study was to ascertain whether **control** in L2 is transfer-induced or whether it arises from general principles, as in L1. Figuring in the research were two kinds of construction – verb complements containing infinitives and those containing (finite) *that*-clauses – and each subcategorized by three verbs: *remind, tell,* and *promise.* The actual sentences with these characteristics (coindexing added here) were the following:

- **Infinitive**
  The worker reminds the woman$_i$ PRO$_i$ to inform the engineer.
  The gentleman tells the teacher$_i$ PRO$_i$ to introduce the owner.
  The lawyer$_i$ promises the doctor PRO$_i$ to prepare the message.

- **Finite *that*-clause**
  The boss$_i$ reminds the man$_j$ that he$_{i,j,k}$ will finish the assignment.
  The owner$_i$ tells the architect$_j$ that he$_{i,j,k}$ will prepare the lunch.
  The owner$_i$ promises the boss$_j$ that he$_{i,j,k}$ will review the test.

Not surprisingly, analogous constructions play out somewhat differently in the three L1s involved. The differences involve what entities can be controllers, the status of infinitives, and whether the three verbs in question can subcategorize [± finite] clausal complements. Details having necessarily to be omitted here, the results of the experiment, consisting of the task of imitating the above six sentences, revealed that transfer did not seem to play a role. All subjects showed a preference for the sentences with non-finite complementation. Imitation of the finite constructions came out in a number of instances as non-finite, though the reverse (non-finites as finites) did not. This occurred despite the fact that neither Chinese nor Japanese has something clearly identifiable as an infinitive, and despite the fact that Spanish *decir* ("tell") and *recordar* ("remind") subcategorize

(continued)

only finite clauses. If L1 transfer can be discounted, then what induced the preference for infinitives over *that*-clauses? The researchers offer a solution arising from the fact that the controller of PRO in infinitives is rooted in a minimal or fixed – i.e. c-command-defined – domain, whereas antecedents for the pronouns in *that*-clauses are not fixed at all (cf. Assignment 94), as in the above examples.

Recall once more from Assignment 31 that children let **minimal distance** over-ride a c-commanding controller in the interpretation of the sentence *The cow kissed the pig$_i$ after* PRO$_i$ *jumping over the fence*. In the research discussed above, however, L2 learners OPTED for clausal alternatives in which (c-commanding) control is crucial. Does this point to an important difference in the two acquisition situations? If not, then in what way(s) can the two be said to be comparable? What additional information concerning coreference in the L2 experiment would enhance the comparability of the two studies?

PART II

Grammatical Operations

SECTION A INFL-Movement

ASSIGNMENT 34* Some Informal Movement Rules in English

Terms referring to rules that serve to move things around in the sentence, or to constructions that are the RESULT of some kind of movement, have long been in use in traditional approaches to grammatical analysis, a good source for which would be Quirk et al. (1985). In many cases the terms themselves are suggestive of **discourse functions** which the rules/constructions are perhaps designed to serve (see Assignment 127). We can conveniently divide these into rules involving **fronting** (movement of an element to the front of the sentence) and **backing** (movement of an element to the end of the sentence).

As for fronting, some requires **inversion** of subject–verb (*Up went the flag*) or of subject–AUX (*where did he ... /never was he ... /so can he ...*). Other fronting requires no inversion and includes both **topicalization** (*Those people I can't stand*) and **left dislocation** (*Those people I can't stand them*).

As for backing, a great deal of it involves so-called **extraposition** and the creation of a **discontinuous dependency** (see Assignment 129). What can be extraposed are **clausal subjects** (*It's good that she writes*), **clausal objects** (*I consider it good that she writes*), **relative clauses** (*the things I mentioned that she writes*), **noun complements** (*What evidence is there that she writes?*), **adjective complements** (*How likely is she to write?*), etc. Other backing is exemplified by **existentials** (*There arose a cloud of dust*), **right dislocation** (*She writes well, that woman*), and **heavy NP shift** (*carrying from the car a large bundle wrapped in plastic*).

Other movement-related phenomena would include the **focus** constructions **cleft** (*It's Mary who writes*/cf. *Mary writes*) and **pseudo-cleft** (*What Mary does is write*/cf. *Mary writes*), **passive** (*The book was written by Mary*/cf. *Mary wrote the book*), and three kinds of **raising: subject-to-subject** (*She appears to write well*/cf. *appear [she to write well]*); **subject-to-object** (*We consider her a good writer*/cf. *We consider [she a good writer]*; **object-to-subject** (*The book was hard to write*/cf. *was hard to write the book*).

The informal movement rules under discussion are outlined on the left below. Next to each rule write the letter of the sentence below them that you think exemplifies it.

(continued)

Fronting
  Without inversion
    Topicalization
      Thematic   1. ...
      Emphatic   2. ...
      Contrastive   3. ...
      Given   4. ...
    Left dislocation   5. ...
  With inversion
    Subject–verb   6. ...
    Subject–AUX
      Interrogatives   7. ...
      Negative   8. ...
      Verb-ing   9. ...
      So   10. ...

Backing
  Extraposition
    of clausal subject   11. ...
    of clausal object   12. ...
    of N complement   13. ...
    of rel. clause/adjunct 14. ...
    of ADJ complement   15. ...
    of comparative   16. ...
  Existential   17. ...
  Right dislocation   18. ...
  Shift   19. ...

Other
  Cleft   20. ...
  Pseudo-cleft   21. ...
  Raising
    Subject-to-subject   22. ...
    Subject-to-object   23. ...
    Object-to-subject   24. ...
  Passive   25. ...

(continued)

Name: _____   Date: __ / __ / __   Class: _____

(a) *Relaxation you call it!*
(b) *What they bought is a Honda*
(c) *Never have we been so angry*
(d) *It's up to you whether we go*
(e) *What business is it of yours?*
(f) *That's hard to believe*
(g) *A choice has been made*
(h) *Where have they gone?*
(i) *There may come a time when ...*
(j) *Rich I may be, but ...*
(k) *How willing is he to help us?*
(l) *She seems to believe it*
(m) *My face I don't mind it*
(n) *Down came the rain*
(o) *He's a clever one, that Jones*
(p) *It's a Honda that she bought*
(q) *So have I*
(r) *... bringing to 23 the number of casualties recorded so far*
(s) *More people own houses now than used to*
(t) *Tomorrow we'll start all over*
(u) *She believes him innocent*
(v) *A problem came up that I had to deal with*
(w) *This subject we've already touched on*
(x) *I leave it to you whether we go*
(y) *Standing in the way was a tree*

ASSIGNMENT **INFL**
35** **(T/AGR)-Movement**

Assume the following analysis for a variety of simple declarative sentences and their corresponding yes/no questions:

(a) T[ense] and AGR[eement] are subsumed under IP

(b) Modals (*can, will, should,* etc.) are subsumed under IP

(c) *be* and (AUX/Aspect) *have* raise to I to acquire their inflectional suffixes – T and AGR

(d) T and AGR otherwise lower to V

(e) I raises to C(omp) for "subject-AUX inversion"

Consider then a sentence like *Has John baked a cake?*, where the VP (*have baked a cake*) contains the main verb *bake*, perfective aspect *have ... -ed*, and the DP *a cake*. Its derivation, invoking (c) and (e) above, would be something like the following, abstracting away some non-essential detail:

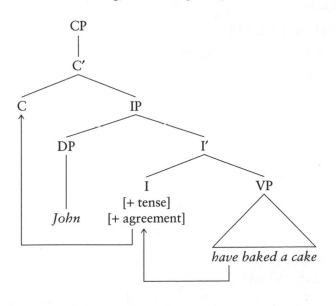

(continued)

For each of the sentences listed below (both grammatical and ungrammatical), state what has happened (or not happened) concerning these facts about movement. Consider only the subordinate clause in nos. 9, 10, 14, 15, and 16.

1.   *He should bake a cake*   *no movement*

2.   *Should he bake a cake?*   *I ("should") raised to C*

3.   *He baked a cake*

4.   **Baked he a cake?*

5.   *He has baked a cake*

6.   *Is he baking a cake?*

7.   **He bake a cake*

8.   **Should he can bake a cake?*

9.   *I wonder if he will bake a cake*

10. **I wonder if will he bake a cake*

11. *Did he bake a cake?*

12. *Had he baked a cake?*

13. **Had he Mary bake a cake?*

14. *If he should bake a cake, we'll eat it*

15. *Should he bake a cake, we'll eat it*

16. **If should he bake a cake, we'll eat it*

17. **He doesn't bakes cakes*

18. *Has he any cake?* [British English]

19. *Does he have any cake?* [American English]

20. **Should they've baked a cake?*

ASSIGNMENT 36** Negation: L1

Refer once more to the sentence-structure analysis presented in the previous assignment. Noting that the location of the subject is Spec, IP, assume (crucially) that it has moved there from its base-generated position of Spec, VP. Although T[ense], AGR[eement], and NEG[ation] assume their own maximal projections (namely, TP, AgrP, NegP) in current work, we will continue to wrap the first two within IP for the sake of convenience. Adding **NegP**, however, will give us a sentence structure something like the following:

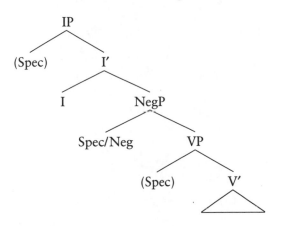

With this kind of analysis in mind, consider the following data of Bellugi (1967) for an early stage of the acquisition of English negation by children:

Not have coffee	*No the sun shining*
No singing song	*No I see truck*
Not write this book	*Not Fraser read it*
No eating that one	*No Mommy giving baby Sarah milk*

Analysis of such data by Bellugi and her colleagues led originally to the conclusion that the children had not yet learned the transformational rule thought then to be required for movement (i.e. lowering) of the negative element from outside to inside the sentence. In more recent work by other researchers, however, it is claimed that the negative elements in these data ARE located inside the sentence

(continued)

– in fact in the same location as in the adult grammar – surface indications to the contrary notwithstanding.

Assuming that IP is the structure represented by each of the above sentences, in what way can it be said that these children already have negation in its proper place? And if it IS in its proper place, what accounts for the differences from adult speech?

ASSIGNMENT 37** Negation: L2

The acquisition of English negation has been examined by a number of SLA researchers over the years. The studies have ranged from childhood to adulthood and over subjects with first languages as diverse as Spanish and Japanese. A brief but useful summary of the findings in this literature is offered in Ellis (1985: 59). Ellis describes, with examples, four stages of acquisition, the first two of which are quoted here:

> Initially, negative utterances are characterized by external negation. That is, the negative particle (usually "no") is attached to a declarative nucleus:

> e.g.   No very good.
>   No you playing here.

> A little later internal negation develops; that is, the negative particle is moved inside the sentence. This often coincides with the use of "not" and/or "don't," which is used variably with "no" as the negative particle . . .

> e.g.   Mariana not coming today.
>   I no can swim.
>   I don't see nothing mop.

Recall that the L1 data from the previous exercise can be analyzed to show that the child already has the negative in its proper position vis-à-vis adult speech. Can the same be said with regard to the above L2 data vis-à-vis target English? Which example would prove problematic for such an analysis and why?

SECTION B **Wh-Movement**

ASSIGNMENT 38* Traces and Antecedents

In the representation of movement transformations, it is always important that the place from which movement took place be marked in some way. One good way of demonstrating the rationale for this can be seen in the derivation of wh-questions with *whom*. A sentence like *Whom shall we ask?* will have a derived structure something like the following:

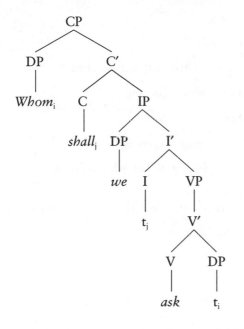

Although *who* would also be grammatical here, *whom* is preferred in many dialects. But *whom*, alone among wh-words, is inflected for case – namely, objective case (cf. **Whom will ask us?*). *Whom* was assigned its case (as well as its theta role – **theme**) at D-structure in its original position as the question word for the object of *ask*. The only way to preserve this information through the movement process – information crucially required for interpretation of the sentence – is to mark the position of extraction with an (empty category) **trace**, usually the letter "t", and to coindex the trace and its antecedent with a

(continued)

subscript (e.g. "i", "j", etc.), one subscript per moved element. Traces thus make it possible to see lexical properties at all levels of derivation, a characteristic that follows from a more general property of grammar termed the **projection principle** (Napoli 1993: 270): "All lexical features of a predicate that appear in DS must appear at every other syntactic level, as well."

In each of the sentences below, insert traces (t) at the ORIGINAL extraction sites of moved wh-elements (if movement has in fact occurred!), underline the element(s) in question (i.e. the antecedent(s)), and coindex each antecedent/trace. For the purposes of this assignment, ignore for now any additional movement such as I to C. Finally, what is unusual about no. 10 and what problem might it pose for trace theory?

For example:

You know <u>what</u>$_i$ I want t_i

1. Tell   me   where   the   concert   is   this   evening

2. What   does   she   think   he   said

3. Who   does   he   think   has   a   hat

4. Tell   me   what   who   said   to   whom

5. Which   one   does   he   think   seems   to   be   the   best

6. When   did   you   say   that   Max   was   coming ⎫
   When   did   you   say   that   Max   was   coming ⎬ [ambiguous]
                                                      ⎭

7. When   did   you   fear · that   Max   was   coming

8. Who   do   you   want   to   teach   [asking about who will do the teaching]

9. You're   thinking   of   taking   a   trip   to   where

10. What   did   you   eat   without   cooking

<u>ASSIGNMENT</u>
39*

I-/Wh-Movement:
L1/L2

Wh-question formation in English invokes two movement operations: in informal terms, fronting of the wh-element and subject–AUX inversion. It is well known that the learner, child as well as adult, cannot initially perform both of these operations simultaneously in order to produce a well-formed question such as *What can John do?* Typically, the first version produced by the learner would be *What John can do?* where wh-movement has applied but not subject–AUX inversion (i.e. I-movement). Note, however, that the theoretically possible version in which I-movement has applied but not wh-movement does NOT occur in learner language. That is, one does not hear *Can John do what?* The interesting question then is why the two rules should seemingly be ordered in this way – namely, wh-movement before I-movement. In considering a possible answer to this question, look again at the tree exemplified in the previous assignment and the trajectories of wh- and I as represented by their traces. Does movement in both cases require the same amount of structural knowledge on the part of the learner?

Name: _____   Date: __ / __ / __   Class: _____

ASSIGNMENT 40** Wh-Movement: L1

Languages are said to differ in terms of whether there is overt wh-movement, as in say English, or whether a wh-word remains in situ, as in say Japanese and Korean. The facts of standard wh-questioning in English are well known and the child apparently need only be exposed to the relevant data in order for learning of these facts to take place and the proper setting of the parameter chosen.

   Now consider the following data:

1. A: I live in the Grand Canyon.
    B: *You live **where**?*

2. A: Do you want to play poker?
    B: *I don't know how.*

3. A: *You know what?* [Cf. *You believe/think/say/etc. what?]
    B: No. What?

What challenges to the child's acquisition of standard English wh-questions can exposure to these kinds of datum (*italicized*) pose? Are the three of equal seriousness? Which of the three can be considered a true **wh-question**?

What additional challenges to the child might be offered upon hearing data like the following:

4. A: *How late it is!*
    B: *How late is it?*

ASSIGNMENT 41* Wh-Movement: L2

The English interlanguage examples listed below contain deviant forms (with respect to the target) that are presumably tied to movement (i.e. V or I) and/ or landing sites. For each *italicized* phrase, state what you think the nature of the deviance is.

1. It is interesting *that how some people learn languages very quickly*

    . . . .

    . . . .

2. Another thing that we don't have is Police inside the university, I couldn't understand *which is their job here*

    . . . .

    . . . .

3. People wonder *how does China with a population of 800 millions could possible be ignored during the last 22 years*

    . . . .

    . . . .

4. While we are surrounded with nothing except atoms, it is interesting to know *what is the structure of an atom*

    . . . .

    . . . .

What kind of movement is plausibly involved in the following IL example?

5. *I* am not possible to know the answer to that

    . . . .

    . . . .

ASSIGNMENT 42*** Wh-Movement (Subjacency)

Movement of various kinds plays an important role in English. In the analysis of a sentence like *What did you ask?*, the questioned element originated as object of *ask* and moved, in its wh- form, to sentence-initial position, as we saw in Assignment 38. The simplified bracketed notation would be

$$[_{CP} \text{ What}_i \text{ did } [_{IP} \text{ you ask } t_i]]$$

where *what* crossed the IP node and landed in the specifier position of CP, leaving a coindexed trace "t" in the extraction site. The bracketed representation of the same sentence with an additional level of embedding, as in *What did you ask if she would say?*, again illustrates this kind of movement:

(a) *What$_i$ did [$_{IP}$ you ask [$_{CP}$ t$_i$ [$_{C'}$ if [$_{IP}$ she would say t$_i$]]]]
     (cf. You asked if she would say X)

Note, however, that the following seemingly similar sentences turn out to be ungrammatical:

(b) **What$_i$ did [$_{IP}$ you ask [$_{CP}$ when [$_{C'}$ e [$_{IP}$ she would say t$_i$]]]]
     (cf. You asked when she would say X)

(c) **What$_i$ did [$_{IP}$ you ask [$_{NP}$ someone [$_{CP}$ who [$_{IP}$ would say t$_i$]]]]
     (cf. You asked someone who would say X)

(d) **What$_i$ did [$_{IP}$ you ask [$_{NP}$ a favor [$_{CP}$ t$_i$ [$_{C'}$ that [$_{IP}$ she should say t$_i$]]]]]
     (cf. You asked a favor that she should say X)

Movement is therefore constrained, bound in fact to the kinds of node that may be crossed in a single step – i.e. **bounding nodes**. Three nodes are at issue here – NP, IP, CP – and subsets of these three constitute the bounding nodes for any language that licenses such overt movement. The nature of this constraint has been formulated as the **subjacency condition** and its application to English is the following:

> Movement cannot cross more than one bounding node in a single step, where the bounding nodes are NP and IP.

(continued)

Note that Spec, CP, serves as an intermediate landing site for the moved wh-, as shown by the middle trace in (a). The reason for the ungrammaticality of examples (b–d) now becomes apparent. In (b) wh-, blocked by *when* from an interim landing, crosses two IPs. In (c) wh-, blocked by *who*, is forced to cross NP and two IPs. In (d) wh-, after an interim landing (note the middle trace), crosses NP and IP.

In each of the sentences below identify the bounding nodes over which wh-movement has occurred and label the relevant brackets accordingly. For the grammatical examples, identify the nodes with comma separation (e.g. NP, IP); for the ungrammatical examples (i.e. where two nodes have been crossed in a single movement), identify them with hyphen separation (e.g. NP-IP). Be prepared to explain the ungrammaticality of the starred examples. Do Nos. 5 and 7 sound less bad and, if so, why? (Look ahead to Assignment 98 for a hint.)

For example:

What did [$_{IP}$ you say [C [$_{IP}$ you wrote ___]]] ......*IP, IP*..

1. *Where do [you want [C [them to be ___]]]* ....

2. *Who do [you want [C [___ to teach]]]* ....

3. *Who did [Max say [C [Lil said [C [you saw ___]]]]]* ....

4. **What do [you like [the idea [C [he's making ___]]]]* ....

5. *?What do [you get [the idea [C [he's making ___]]]]* ....

6. *What did [you claim [C [he said ___]]]* ....

7. *?What did [you make [the claim [that [he said ___]]]]* ....

8. **What did [you file [the claim [that [he said ___]]]]* ....

9. *It's a road [which [I don't know ___]]* ....

10. **It's a road [which [I don't know [where [___ goes]]]* ....

11. **Where would [[for [us to live ___]] please them]* ....

12. *Who did [you say [C [you heard [that [she said all those things to ___]]]]]* ....

13. *Whose kids did [letters to him upset ___]* ....

14. **Whose kids did [[letters to ___] upset him]* ....

15. *Whose kids did [[letters to ___] upset ___]* ....

ASSIGNMENT 43** Wh-Movement (Subjacency): L2

Recall from the previous assignment that the **subjacency condition** applies to languages that exhibit overt wh-movement. Not all languages in fact have this feature, however. Among the well-known languages that do not license such movement would be Chinese. Repeated here from the discussion portion of the previous assignment (with some needed modification) are examples (a)–(c) and a necessary reformulation of (d), together with their Chinese counterparts:

(a) *What$_i$ did he ask if you would say t$_i$?*

    ta wen ni   shi-bu-shi shuo le   shenme
    he ask you be-not-be say Asp what

    "He asked if you said what (something)"

(b) * *What$_i$ did he ask when you would say t$_i$*

    ta wen ni   shenme shihou shuo le   shenme
    he ask you what   time   say Asp what

    "He asked you said what what time"

(c) * *What$_i$ did he ask a person who would say t$_i$*

    ta wen le   shuo shenme de ren
    he ask Asp say   what   DE person

(d) * *What$_i$ did he hear the rumor that you said t$_i$*

    ta tingdao ni   shuo shenme DE yaoyan
    he hear   you say   what   DE rumor

It is readily apparent that the four examples above are grammatical in Chinese, including all three whose English counterparts violate subjacency and are therefore UNgrammatical. What kinds of subjacency effect might then plausibly obtain for language learning in adulthood and what might one conclude from them?

                                                     (continued)

Name: _____   Date: __ / __ / __   Class: _____

For the purposes of this assignments, assume the following:

- that the subjacency condition is part of Universal Grammar (UG)

- that we have a language contact situation in which the L1 does not exhibit overt wh-movement at all (e.g. Chinese, as in the above examples) and the L2 does (e.g. English)

- that the L2 learners already know the syntactic constructions that figure in examples (a)–(d)

- that one can test empirically for knowledge of L2 (un)grammaticality effects with reference to subjacency

What preliminary conclusions could one reasonbly draw vis-à-vis L2 access to UG and based on whether or not the L2 learner consistently identified correctly or incorrectly the grammaticalness of examples like (a)–(d)?

ASSIGNMENT
44***

Wh-Movement
(Asymmetry): L2

English reveals a certain asymmetry with regard to extraction phenomena. That is, wh-extraction from within a CP complement of a verb is possible from object position but not subject position:

(a) (i) *Who_i do you think* [_CP *that Mary saw* t_i]?
    (ii) **Who_i do you think* [_CP *that* t_i *saw Mary*]?

In Dutch, such wh-extraction is possible from BOTH positions:

(b) (i) *Wie_i zei Mary* [_CP *dat* t_i *het glas gebroken heeft*]?
        who said Mary   that   the glass broken   has
        "Who did Mary say broke the glass?"

    (ii) *Wat_i denk je*   [_CP *dat Mary zal doen* t_i]?
        what think you   that Mary will do
        "What do you think that Mary will do?"

Since Dutch learners of English can identify the ungrammaticality of sentences like (a(ii)), it has been claimed that this can be taken as evidence for the operation of UG in SLA (i.e. learner knowledge of the so-called **Empty Category Principle** – namely, that traces of moved elements must be properly governed). That is, since knowledge of such ungrammaticality could not have derived from the native language (or, in this instance, corrective feedback), UG is the only other possible source.

Jordens (1991), however, has argued that an explanation for the correct grammaticality judgments by Dutch learners for examples (a(i)/(ii)) need not appeal to UG. Contrary to the claim above, it WOULD be possible, for example, to predict the judgments for (a(i)/(ii)) on the basis of transfer from Dutch. Relevant to such an accounting is the fact that Dutch canonical word order is SOV.

(continued)

Therefore, both **subject** and **object extraction** in Dutch result in an **NP V** construction: SOV → OV or SV

But in English, **object extraction** results in **NP V**:   SVO → SV
whereas **subject extraction** results in   **V NP**:   SVO → VO

Using only the data supplied above, how then (very briefly!) might one arrive at an accounting of these learner judgments based only on transfer?

SECTION C Raising

ASSIGNMENT 45* Raising vs. Control (I)

Sentences like *They V to be noticed* are analyzable in terms of a main verb that requires one of two kinds of predicate:

(a) **control**: *They$_i$ want* [$_{CP}$ C PRO$_i$ *to be noticed*]

where the main-verb subject *they* **controls**, or is interpreted as, understood subject – i.e. **PRO** (Assignment 30) – in the CP complement ... *to be noticed* ...

(b) **raising**: [$_{DP}$ e] *tend* [$_{IP}$ *They to be noticed*]

where the main-verb subject *they* has been **raised** from subject of the IP complement *they to be noticed* ... , leaving a trace t:

$$\rightarrow [_{DP} \textit{They}_i] \textit{ tend } [_{IP} \text{ t}_i \textit{ to be noticed}]$$

Want is therefore said to be a control verb, *tend* a raising verb. (Motivation for raising is addressed in Assignment 71.)

Some tests that are useful in determining whether a complement-taking verb is of the control or raising type are the following:

- existential *there*:
  There **wants to be a problem / There **tends** to be a problem*

- selectional data:
  *John/his cat/?his car/??his life/*his toothbrush [**wants** to be noticed]*
  *John/his cat/his car/his life/his toothbrush/etc. [**tends** to be noticed]*

- active/passive (non-)equivalence:
  *He **wants** to be noticed by everyone ≠ Everyone **wants** to notice him*
  *He **tends** to be noticed by everyone = Everyone **tends** to notice him*

Applying one or more of the diagnostics just cited, check the verbs below for membership in the control or the raising categories.

(continued)

Name: _____ Date: __ / __ / __ Class: _____

			Control	Raising
1.	He tends	to be liked by everybody	. . .	✓ .
2.	wants		✓ .	. . .
3.	seems		. . .	. . .
4.	expects		. . .	. . .
5.	continues		. . .	. . .
6.	likes		. . .	. . .
7.	began		. . .	. . .
8.	's going		. . .	. . .
9.	hoped		. . .	. . .
10.	used		. . .	. . .
11.	happens		. . .	. . .
12.	prefers		. . .	. . .
13.	came		. . .	. . .
14.	has		. . .	. . .
15.	fails		. . .	. . .
16.	tries		. . .	. . .
17.	started		. . .	. . .
18.	appears		. . .	. . .
19.	strives		. . .	. . .
20.	needs		. . .	. . .

<hr/>

ASSIGNMENT
46**

Raising vs.
Control (II)

The sentences below contain more than one instance of a raising and/or control predicate. Represent in brackets, and with coindexing, that portion of the derived structure occurring as (*italicized*) infinitival complement to the main verb.
   For example:

He seems [*to tend to need help*]
He$_i$ seems [$_{IP}$ t$_i$ to tend [$_{IP}$ t$_i$ to need help]]

He used [*to expect to have help*]
He$_i$ used [$_{IP}$ t$_i$ to expect [$_{CP}$ C PRO$_i$ to have help]]

1. He seems [*to want to help*]

. . . .

2. He wants [*to seem to need help*]

. . . .

3. He would like [*there to seem to be no problem*]

. . . .

4. He doesn't want [*it to continue to be windy*]

. . . .

5. He has [*to try to start to appear to know something*]

. . . .

ASSIGNMENT 47* Verb Raising

The tree below for the sentence *John doesn't often bake cakes* is identical to the tree displayed in Assignment 35 except that CP has been given more internal structure and two more constituents have been added:

- The negative *not* heads another phrasal projection: **NegP**, as seen in Assignment 36.

- VP adverbials, as represented by *often, always, quickly, quietly*, etc., appear as ADV **adjunctions** to the VP.

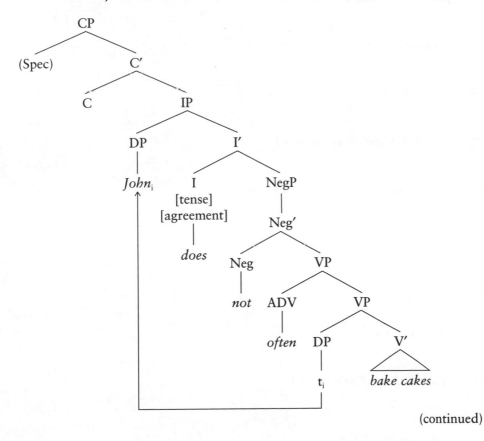

(continued)

With respect to the verbal elements, state what might be happening, or not happening, in the derivation of the following constructions. Some of the ungrammatical items are typical of certain L2 English learner production.

1. *John doesn't be happy

    "Be" must raise . . . .

2. *John does not have gone

    . . . .

3. Do you have any money?

    . . . .

4. Have you any money? [British English]

    . . . .

5. *John eats quickly dinner

    . . . .

6. John should quickly eat dinner

    . . . .

7. Shouldn't John quickly eat dinner?

    . . . .

8. for me to leave

    . . . .

9. John completely lost his mind

    . . . .

10. *John completely will lose his mind

    . . . .

11. John quietly left

    . . . .

12. *Left John?

    . . . .

13. *John not left

    . . . .

14. *John always didn't study

    . . . .

<u>ASSIGNMENT</u>
48** Verb Raising and Adverb Placement: L2

The following data for adverb placement in French and English are taken from White (1991a), where the parenthesized abbreviations refer to S(ubject), V(erb), A(dverb), O(bject), and P(repositional) P(hrase):

(a)   *Jean regarde souvent la télévision* (SVAO)

(b)   **John watches often television* (SVAO)

(c)   **Marie souvent regarde la télévision* (SAVO)

(d)   *Mary often watches television* (SAVO)

(e)   *John walks quickly to school* (SVAPP)

These word-order differences are claimed to be traceable to whether or not the language in question allows main verbs to **raise**, offered as a parametric difference among languages. French verbs raise to INFL, carrying them to the left of VP adverbs, as in (a); English main verbs do not raise and thus occur to the right of VP adverbs, as in (d); the ordering in (e) comes about via base generation of V PP A and movement of PP to sentence-final position. (Knowledge of the complex details of the raising analysis and its ramifications (cf. Pollock 1989) is not essential for the purposes of this assignment.)

White experimented with French-speaking children aged 11–12 in an ESL setting, with an experimental group (I) given instruction (including negative evidence) on English adverb placement and a comparison group (II) instructed only on English question formation. The researcher found that the experimental group accepted/produced and rejected English sentences according to the pattern below, where starred items are the rejections:

Before instruction (I and II):	*SAV(O)	SVAO	
After adverb-placement instruction (I):	SAV	*SVAO	*SVAPP
Without adverb-placement instruction (II):	*SAV	SVAO	SVAPP
One year after instruction (I):	*SAV(O)	SVAO	

(continued)

Putting aside for now other details of the research design and such questions as the KIND of formal instruction administered, what brief comments might be made about the role of positive and negative evidence in L2 in light of the fact that group I judged both SVAO and SVAPP to be ungrammatical after adverb-placement instruction and reverted to the original grammaticality judgments one year after instruction? If the contrasting verb-raising facts for English and French are an instance of contrasting settings on a "verb-raising" parameter in UG, what implications could the experimental results have for the notion of "resetting" the parameter in the course of L2 learning?

SECTION D Relativization

ASSIGNMENT 49*   Relative Clause: Characteristics

At least five kinds of construction have been cited as examples of modification of a noun in the form of **relativization** (for which a good descriptive source would be Quirk et al. 1985):

- restrictive relative:
  *The bus **that I took** is no. 7*

- non-restrictive relative:
  *Bus no. 7, **which I didn't take**, doesn't go there*

- free (headless) relative:
  ***What I took** isn't important*

- participial relative:
  *The bus **arriving late** is no. 7*

- infinitival relative:
  *The first bus **(for NP) to take** is no. 7*
  *The first bus   **to come** was no. 7*

The type that has figured most prominently in the acquisition literature and that will therefore concern us throughout this section is the **restrictive relative**. Some general facts about this kind of relativization are illustrated below through examples of the limitations on its internal structure:

(a) Relativizing on the **subject**
      *That's the person **that/who gave me the book***
      cf. [___ *gave me the book*]
      That's the person ___ *gave me the book

(b) Relativizing on **other than the subject**
      *That's the book **(that/which)** I gave (to) the person*
      cf. [*I gave* ___ *to the person*]
          [*I gave the person* ___]

      *That's the person **(that/who/whom)** I gave the book (to)*
      cf. [*I gave the book to* ___]
          [*I gave* ___ *the book*]

                                                              (continued)

(b)(i)   With **fronting of a preposition** ("pied-piping")
       *That's the person **to** *that/*who/whom I gave the book*

(b)(ii)   Relativizing on a **possessive**
       *That's the person **whose** book I borrowed*
       cf. [*I borrowed ___'s book*]

Each of the sentences listed below contains at least one **restrictive relative clause**. Put brackets around the clause(s) and underline the noun phrase(s) with which the clause(s) are in construction (i.e. the noun phrases which they modify).

1.   He was a star in the Clinton cabinet, the darling of the media, and . . . had just been contacted about the first vacancy Clinton would fill on the Supreme Court. (*Sierra*, July/August 1994: 55)

2.   [The fabulous mechanical duck] could perform the amazing feat of drinking water and eating grain which was digested and then excreted via a mysterious chemical process. (G. Yule, *The Study of Language*, p. 115)

3.   The Steve I know wouldn't have been capable of doing those killings. (*New Yorker*, June 13, 1994: 46)

4.   Proposition 177 allows commercial and residential property owners to make renovations that improve access for disabled individuals without raising property taxes. (California Ballot Pamphlet, June 7, 1994: 5)

5.   . . . the largest molecule we know and the smallest living particles we know overlap. (N. Chomsky, *Knowledge of Language*, p. xix)

6.   Whenever Bach writes an obbligato for the bassoon he underlines its tender qualities, and the relatively few occasions when it is written for in this manner must be an indication that he rarely encountered a player worthy of him. (W.G. Whittaker, *The Cantatas of Johann Sebastian Bach*, vol. 1, p. 55)

7.   Anyone who will listen carefully to ordinary conversation will come across abundant evidence of the way in which sentences are built up gradually by the speaker. (O. Jespersen, *The Philosphy of Grammar*, p. 28)

8.   There seems to be even more to it than that, according to a pretty broad hint I got one day from the proprietor of my favourite restaurant in Brussels; a hint which made me think of Opie's famous answer, "With brains, sir", when some one asked him how he mixed his colours. (A.J. Nock, *Memoirs of a Superfluous Man*, pp. 142–3)

9.   As to the cigarette tax, the reason it's appropriate to single out tobacco is that cigarettes are the only products which, when used as intended, cause disease and death. (*Los Angeles Times*, June 25, 1994: B7)

10.   Here was the medical community . . . actively advocating megadose vitamin therapy for a condition I was very personally interested in. (R.E. Kowalski, *The 8-Week Cholesterol Cure*, p. 57)

ASSIGNMENT **Relative Clause**
50* **(Shared-Noun Relationship)**

In each of the following examples, identify the relative clause and put brackets [ ] around it. Then indicate the surface syntactic relation (subject or object) of the shared NP to the verb (or preposition) in the matrix clause and the verb (or preposition) in the constituent (i.e. relative) clause, and in that order. Use the abbreviations S-O, S-S, O-S, O-O. Let O stand for any relationship other than S.
  For example:

.*SS*. People [who live in glass houses] shouldn't throw stones
          S   S

.*OS*. I don't know any people [who live in glass houses]
          O   S

1. . . . . . Has anybody seen the notebook I left on the table?

2. . . . . . Who do you know who's better than you are?

3. . . . . . Out of the bushes jumped a guy that everybody recognized

4. . . . . . This book is for everybody who writes

5. . . . . . The woman who has everything is hard to buy a gift for

6. . . . . . We believe the man to be innocent who others accuse of the crime

(continued)

7. . . . . . *A person whom you think you can't trust is probably not trustworthy*

8. . . . . . *He who laughs last laughs best*

9. . . . . . *They brought up a subject that nobody else had been willing to talk about*

10. . . . . . *Can you think of a word that begins with X?*

11. . . . . . *What bothers you that you tried to call me about?*

12. . . . . . *We need above all a contractor that we can rely on*

13. . . . . . *A man came into the room who was wearing funny clothes*

14. . . . . . *They told us about some great wines that were worth hopping aboard a time machine and hurrying back to sample*

15. . . . . . *One of the most common things that nobody likes is taxes*

Name: ______________________________ Date: __/__/__ Class: ______________

ASSIGNMENT

51* Relative Clause (Shared-Noun Relationship): L1/L2

Language acquisition researchers have suggested that children tend to make use of certain "strategies" in the comprehension and production of relative clauses. One of these – the **Parallel-Function Strategy** (Sheldon 1977) – states roughly that children will prefer (i.e. find it easier to process) relativization in which the head noun bears an identical relationship (i.e. **subject, object**) to the verbs in the matrix (main) clause and in the constituent (relative) clause. Another of these – the **Adjacency Strategy** (cf. Slobin 1971; Sheldon 1977) – states roughly that children will prefer relativization in which the constituent clause occurs adjacent to, rather than embedded within, the matrix clause.

Consider the following four examples of relativization, where the grammatical function (subject or object) of the head noun vis-à-vis both matrix and constituent clause is indicated by combinations of S and O:

The students that passed the test studied hard (SS)
***The students** [**The students** passed the test] studied hard*
S S

The test that the students took was hard (SO)
***The test** [The students took **the test**] was hard*
S O

The students passed the test that they took (OO)
*The students passed **the test** [They took **the test**]*
O O

The students took a test that was hard (OS)
*The students took **a test** [**The test** was hard]*
O S

Taking the above two strategies together, consider what order of (**processing**) difficulty could be predicted for these four types of relative clause. Using the S/O abbreviations and plotting an increase in difficulty from left to right, we

(continued)

would have something like the following, where SS/OS are of equal difficulty and thus not ordered:

$$OO > SS/OS > SO$$

Subsequent research, however, has called into question the validity of predictions arising from utilization of the Parallel-Function Strategy. Figuring more prominently, it would seem, is the fact that subjects (S) are more **accessible** (i.e. easier to process) that objects (O). This can be illustrated by the number of discontinuities created by relativizing on these two positions:

relativized S: *the students who$_i$ [$_{IP}$ t$_i$ took the test]*
relativized O: *the test which$_i$ [$_{IP}$ the students [$_{VP}$ took t$_i$]]*

Thus, **relativized S**, which contains only one discontinuity – namely, IP – should be easier to process than **relativized O**, which contains two – IP and VP.

Taking this observation in combination with the above Adjacency Strategy, consider again the order of processing difficulty predictable for these same four types of relative clause: SS, SO, OO, OS. For ease of exposition, the four types can be plotted vis-à-vis the three strategies in the following manner (where, for discontinuity, "+" = one and "–" = two):

	SS	SO	OO	OS
parallel function:	+	–	+	–
adjacency:	–	–	+	+
discontinuity:	+	–	–	+

As already noted, the order of difficulty predicted by the Parallel Function and Adjacency Strategies would be the following:

$$OO > SS/OS > SO$$

What then would be the order of difficulty predicted by the Adjacency Strategy in combination with the discontinuity observations:

. . . . . > . . . . . > . . . . . > . . . . .

Which relative clause type is predicted by AIL THREE strategies to be the most difficult?

. . . .

ASSIGNMENT 52** Relative Clause vs. Noun Complement vs. Cleft Sentence

There are three constructions, among others in English, that bear superficial similarity but underlying differences – namely, **relative clause, noun complement,** and **cleft sentence.** The surface similarity is obvious in examples like the following, where the bracketed portion identifies the construction:

■ relative clause:
   *There's a big claim [**that he filed**]*

■ **noun complement:**
   *There's a big claim [**that he failed**]*

■ cleft sentence:
   *[**It's a big claim that he filed**] not a complaint*

Although both the relative clause and the noun complement are modifiers of the NP to which they attach – e.g. *big claim* in the above examples – in phrase structure terms the relative clause is an **adjunct,** the noun complement (obviously) a **complement** (Assignment 7). The cleft sentence is a construction of emphasis or **focus,** equivalent in the above example to *He filed a big claim,* where the element focused upon (in this case for contrast) is *big claim.*

   Although the seemingly very similar relative clause and noun complement have the greater potential for confusion, they can readily be distinguished in terms of both structure and intonation.

● **structure:**   Only the relative clause is linked to the modified element via a "shared noun" (Assignment 50), which can appear as a moved wh- word leaving a trace:
              *There's a big claim (**which**$_i$) he filed   t$_i$*
                                    (He filed a big claim)
           There's a big claim **which he failed*
                                    (*He failed a big claim)
                                                      (continued)

145

- **intonation:** In something approaching a discourse-neutral setting, relative clause intonation will peak on the shared NP; noun complement intonation will peak somewhere AFTER the NP:

There's a big claim that he filed

There's a big claim that he failed

In each of the examples listed below, look for and identify relative clauses (RC), noun complements (NC), and cleft sentence constructions (CS). If the example contains more than one such construction, identify them in the order in which their left-most boundary occurs. If the example contains none of these, write Ø. Put brackets [ ] around the construction(s) in question.

1. . *RC* . *Where's the truck [that he bought?]*

2. . . . . . *It's a car that he bought, not a truck*

3. . . . . . *The idea that he would buy a truck is ridiculous*

4. . . . . . *It's that he bought a Yugo that surprises me*

5. . . . . . *It's the Yugo that he bought that died, not the VW*

6. . . . . . *This is the Yugo that he bought*

7. . . . . . *This is the evidence that he bought a Yugo*

8. . . . . . *This is the evidence that they presented that he bought a Yugo*

9. . . . . . *Where is it written in the book that syntax is autonomous?*

10. . . . . . *Where is the notion that syntax is autonomous actually written?*

11. . . . . . *Where does it say that it's syntax that's autonomous?*

12. . . . . . *Where's the book that says that syntax is autonomous?*

13. . . . . . *Where is the evidence for the solution that you came up with?*

14. . . . . . *"[They] provide a useful descriptive framework for the hypothesis presented in this paper – that it is the commonality of features on case values that are given case values that are missing that enables one to make inferences across sentence boundaries"* (Finn: SWRL Professional Paper #40, p. 63)

15. . . . . . *"It is the high pricetag stores such as Bergdorf Goodman, a division of Federated Department Stores Inc., of Cincinnati, and the discount and off-price retailers such as Mervyn's, a division of Dayton-Hudson Co. of Minneapolis, and Caldor, the New England-based retailer that recently agreed to merge with New York-based Associated Dry Goods Inc., that have posted double digit sales increases in the first two months of 1981"* (Los Angeles Times)

Name: _____   Date: __ / __ / __   Class: _____

Relative Clause, Noun Complement, Infinitival: L2

Among the five kinds of construction cited as examples of relativization in Assignment 49 was one labeled **infinitival relative**, as in *the first bus to come (was no. 7)*, roughly equivalent in meaning to "the first bus **that came** . . ."

Although the **noun complement** constructions encountered in the previous assignment were of the finite variety, these too can also be infinitival, as in *the need **to help**, a plan **to succeed**, the decision **to leave**,* etc.

Native-speaking Chinese learners of L2 English produce an abundance of somewhat ungrammatical sentences like the following, documented in Yip (1995):

*There is two kinds of **people to visit the museum**.*

*There is a **cascade to drop down the river**.*

*Without limitation, there will be a lot of **foreign students to come here** and never return to their home countries.*

*There are many **reasons to result in a crime**.*

*There are many **things . . . to cause cancer**.*

From an analytical standpoint, which of the two constructions – infinitival relative or infinitival complement – do the Chinese IL examples resemble more, and why? Assuming that the L2 learning continues, what would you predict as the most likely target English structure to emerge from the above infinitivals?

ASSIGNMENT 54* Relative Clause: Representation

Refer once more to the facts of relative clause formation outlined in Assignment 49. For the purpose of illustrating these constructions quasi-formally, we will use the **object relative**. Observe that from the sentence *I put the book on the table* it is possible, relativizing on the noun *book*, to produce three different versions:

(a)   *the book **which** I put on the table*
(b)   *the book   I put on the table*
(c)   *the book **that**   I put on the table*

A simplified tree-template for all three, abstracting away non-essential detail, would be the following:

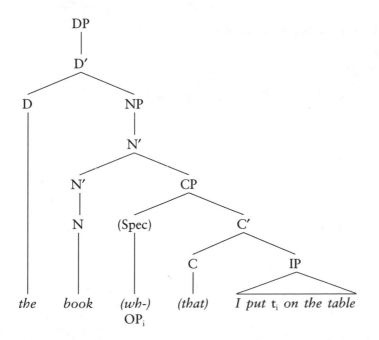

(continued)

149

As in all **overt** wh-movement (Assignment 38), *which* in (a) moves to Spec, CP, leaving the trace:

the book [$_{CP}$ **which**$_i$ [$_C$ e] [$_{IP}$ *I put* t$_i$ *on the table*]]

In (b), wh-movement is **covert**, where the null **operator**, represented as **OP**, in a sense stands in for the moved wh-:

the book [$_{CP}$ **OP**$_i$ [$_C$ e] [$_{IP}$ *I put* **t**$_i$ *on the table*]]

In (c), wh-movement is again covert but the **complementizer** *that* is now realized as **head** of CP:

the book [$_{CP}$ **OP**$_i$ [$_C$ **that**] [$_{IP}$ *I put* t$_i$ *on the table*]]

   With respect to the bracketing conventions outlined above, provide a similarly simplified labeled-bracket representation of each of the following *italicized* relative clauses:

1. the table *that I put the book on*

2. the table *on which I put the book*

3. the person *who put the book on the table*

4. the person *that I asked to put the book on the table*

5. the book *she forgot the title of*

6. the book *whose title she forgot*

<hr>
ASSIGNMENT
55*

Relative Clause: Resumptive Pronouns and L2

In the production data of adult L2 English interlanguage (IL), the researcher often encounters sentences containing apparent relative clauses (RCs) with so-called **resumptive pronouns** – e.g. *the man that I saw **him***. With reference to wh-movement, what kind of RC analysis would make the most sense for an IL corpus all of whose relativization data were like the following:

> *the man that I saw **him***
> *the man that **he** saw me*
> *the man that I bought **his** car*
> *the man that I gave some money **to him***
>   *... that ...*
>   *... that ...*

Would adjustments be required if additional IL production by the same learner occasionally revealed examples like the following:

> *the man **who** I saw him*
> *the man **who** I gave some money to him*

<table>
<tr><td>ASSIGNMENT
56**</td><td># Relative Clause:
Ungrammaticality</td></tr>
</table>

ASSIGNMENT 56** Relative Clause: Ungrammaticality

For most native speakers of English, the sentences below are ungrammatical. The ungrammaticality in each case results from a contravention of something concerning relativization that can be found in the following list, cross-referenced to the previous assignment where it was introduced:

(a) **absence of complementizer or wh-word in subject relative**
     (Assignment 49, example (a))

(b) **subjacency violation**
     (Assignment 42)

(c) **pied-piping with complementizer**
     (Assignment 49, example b(i))

(d) **pied-piping of complement preposition or particle**
     (Assignment 27)

(e) **wrong case assignment by preposition**
     (Assignment 49, example b(i))

Write the letter ((a) through (e)) corresponding to the error. (Note that a sentence may contain more than one violation.)

1. .... *The hat on which you should put is the warm one.
2. .... *She served something that for John to eat would make him sick.
3. .... *She served something that John got sick after he ate.
4. .... *Where's the light switch off that I'm supposed to turn?
5. .... *The horse lost the race fell.
6. .... *Who's the person to who I should speak?
7. .... *We saw a game that the end of was dramatic.
8. .... *They gave me a question the answer to that nobody knew.
9. .... *There's somebody wants to see you.
10. .... *Ending a sentence with a preposition is something up with which I will not put. [Winston Churchill]

Name: _____   Date: __/__/__   Class: _____

ASSIGNMENT 57*** Relative Clause (Adjunction vs. Conjunction): L1

It has been suggested that the structure of relative clauses represents cross-linguistically a binary choice, formulated (using earlier phrase-structure termino-logy) as a UG parameter: either **adjoin** the clause (= CP) to the head NP or **conjoin** the clause to IP:

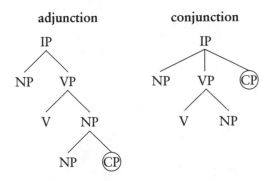

Hittite, according to Vainikka (1990), is an example of relative clause **conjunction** and English of **adjunction**. It has been claimed (Lebeaux 1990), on the basis of L1 acquisition data, that conjunction is the default – i.e. that the adjunction setting will require positive evidence. The question then arises of what might constitute evidence that could lead the child learning English to adopt the adjunction setting. Lebeaux (1990) suggests that exposure to a sentence like the following would be such an example:

The lion put the turtle that saw the fish in the trunk

How then can this sentence be taken as evidence for the need to **adjoin** rather than **conjoin** relative clauses in English? In the two trees sketched above, attach the extra constituent needed to represent this sentence – namely the verb-complement PP (*in the trunk*) – and map the lexicon of the entire sentence under the corresponding nodes in both trees. Briefly, what problem arises in the case of **conjunction**?

SECTION E Contraction and Cliticization

_____
ASSIGNMENT **Contraction:**

58*   *have* and *be*

All of the examples below display **contraction** in English with *be* and *have*. Some of these are grammatical; some are ungrammatical; and the grammatical status of still others – nos. 5, 6, and 7 – likely splits along dialect lines (i.e. British vs. American English). For each contraction, write the word (*be* or *have*) that has been contracted. For the ungrammatical (starred) examples, write the word whose full form (*be* or *have*) would render the sentence grammatical.

1. .... *He's contacted every day*

2. .... *He's contacted us every day*

3. .... *He's to contact us*

4. .... *He's been contacted*

5. .... *?She's a lot of money in the bank*

6. .... *?She's a cut on her finger*

7. .... *?She's a car at her disposal*

8. .... **He's a party every night*

9. .... *He's a party animal*

10. .... **She's a baby every twelve months*

11. .... *She's a baby-boomer*

12. .... **He's her friend pick him up*

13. .... *He's her friend*

(continued)

What observations can be made on the basis of these examples? Are there any ungrammatical sentences with *be*? What features would you say *have* displays across the three groups? Note the correlation between the distribution of *have* as shown in the above examples and the (im)possibilities of attaching question tags (cf. Assignment D).

ASSIGNMENT
59**

Contraction:
Traces

It was noted in the previous assignment that contraction with *be* is unrestricted. Although this is true for the kinds of example cited, restrictions do apply as the result of certain grammatical operations. Consider the following contrasting pairs, where contraction blocks in (i) but not in (ii):

(a) (i)   *Tell me where the concert's this evening*
     (ii)   *The concert's this evening*

(b) (i)   *I know how happy **he's** in his new apartment*
     (ii)   ***He's** in his new apartment*

(c) (i)   *I wonder what the **answer's** in the back of the book*
     (ii)   *The **answer's** in the back of the book*

(d) (i)   *Sally's more dependable than **Carrie's***
     (ii)   ***Carrie's** dependable*

(e) (i)   *Sally's as happy at work as **Carrie's** at home*
     (ii)   ***Carrie's** at home*
        (*Sally's as happy at work as Carrie's content at home*)

(f) (i)   *Sally's thin and **Carrie's** too*
     (ii)   ***Carrie's** thin too*
        (*Sally's thin and so's Carrie*)

Consider also the following examples with *want to* and *have to*:

(g) *What do they* $\left\{\begin{array}{l}\textit{want to}\\\textit{wanna}\end{array}\right\}$ *read?*

(h) *What do they* $\left\{\begin{array}{l}\textit{want to}\\\textit{*wanna}\end{array}\right\}$ *happen?*

(i) *What did they* $\left\{\begin{array}{l}\textit{have to}\\\textit{hafta}\end{array}\right\}$ *fix?*

(j) *What did they* $\left\{\begin{array}{l}\textit{have to}\\\textit{*hafta}\end{array}\right\}$ *fix it?*

(continued)

Briefly, what can one say accounts for the grammaticality differences between the above pairs? It will help to refer once more to Assignment 38.

<hr>

ASSIGNMENT **Contraction:**
60* **General**

Contraction in all the sentences below is presumed to be disallowed. Some of the ungrammaticality has been presented in the previous two assignments. For each example, state briefly what you think has prevented contraction from occurring.
  For example:

　　　*John's as easy to talk to as Mary's to write to. (*is*)

　　　deletion of "easy" following "is" . . . .

1.　*We'd them put the furniture in the living room. (*had*)

. . . .

2.　*They're'nt sure. (*not*)

. . . .

3.　*Can you tell me where the meeting's? (*is*)

. . . .

4.　*He's as bad as I'm. (*am*)

. . . .

5.　*Should we've called the police? (*have*)

. . . .

6.　*John's problem isn't knowing what to do. (*not*)
　　(I.e. He doesn't know what to do and that is his problem.)

. . . .

7.　*I've been to New York as often as I've to London. (*have*)

. . . .

8.　*They'd measles before they were ten. (*had*)

. . . .

(continued)

9. *Who has he **gotta** fix it? (got to)

. . . .

10. *They each'd had measles before they were ten. (had)

. . . .

11. *The thing he should have remembered wasn't to worry. (not)
    (I.e. He shouldn't have worried.)

. . . .

12. *Would you've wanted to be invited? (have)

. . . .

ASSIGNMENT 61** Cliticization

Note these definitions:

- **encliticization** (encl): attachment to the END of the PRECEDING word
- **procliticization** (procl): attachment to the BEGINNING of the FOLLOWING word

Now consider these examples:

(a) *John thinks I should leave, but I don't* $\begin{cases} want\ to\ \emptyset\ \text{(i)} \\ wanna\quad \emptyset\ \text{(ii)} \end{cases}$

(b) *I wonder where* $\begin{cases} John\ is\ \emptyset\ \text{(i)} \\ *John's\ \emptyset\ \text{(ii)} \end{cases}$

Thus, if (a(ii)) is possible, then why not also (b(ii))?
   A similar contrast is evident in (c) and (d), which are structurally the same in the relevant aspects:

(c) *Who do you* $\begin{cases} think\ is\ here\ \text{(i)} \\ think's\ here\quad \text{(ii)} \end{cases}$

   Who do you think [___ is here]

(d) *Who do you* $\begin{cases} want\ to\ be\ here\ \text{(i)} \\ *wanna\ be\ here\quad \text{(ii)} \end{cases}$

   Who do you want [___ to be here]

(continued)

State briefly what accounts for the facts of contraction among these data, in terms of the two kinds of cliticization cited above.

ASSIGNMENT 62**

Cliticization: L1

Consider again the cliticization data from the previous exercise. State briefly how the child learning English could achieve criterion for this portion of the grammar without negative evidence. That is, which of the grammatical exemplars displayed can serve as positive evidence for excluding the ungrammatical ones? Crucial to this question is the fact that cliticization requires that the cliticized items be adjacent.

ASSIGNMENT 63*   Contraction/Deletion: Dialects

Certain kinds of contraction and deletion are possible in varieties of American English. The following examples illustrate some of these possibilities (and imposs-ibilities) for one very common dialect:

Have you seen any good movies lately?
    'vyou seen any good movies lately?
      You seen any good movies lately?
          Seen any good movies lately?
*Have   seen any good movies lately?

Do you think it's gonna rain?   *Did you think it was gonna rain?*
  D'you think it's gonna rain?   *Dj'you think it was gonna rain?*
    You think it's gonna rain?   **You think it was gonna rain? [past]*
      Think it's gonna rain?   **Think it was gonna rain? [past]*
*Do   think it's gonna rain? **Did   think it was gonna rain?*

Are you waiting for the bus?
  'ryou waiting for the bus?
    You waiting for the bus?
      Waiting for the bus?
*Are   waiting for the bus?

Very briefly, what generalizations account for the grammatical and ungram-matical sequences?

(continued)

169

It has been noted that many forms of **Black English (BE)**, in contrast to **Standard English (SE)**, allow **declarative** sentences of the form

You waiting for the bus.

How would BE examples like this be related to your generalization above?

PART III

Grammatical Relations

SECTION A **Thematic Relations**

ASSIGNMENT 64* Theta-Roles

Thematic- or **theta**-roles are idealizations of **thematic relations**. The following definitions of the various theta-roles are taken from Cowper (1992), Haegeman (1994), and O'Grady et al. (1989):

AGENT – the entity that initiates the action

THEME – the affected entity (e.g. undergoing an action or change of state, or coming into being); also pure existence

GOAL – the entity toward which motion (concrete or abstract) takes place

SOURCE – the entity from which motion (concrete or abstract) takes place

EXPERIENCER – the entity that feels or perceives something

STIMULUS – the entity that is perceived

INSTRUMENT – the entity with which an action is carried out

BENEFICIARY – the entity for whose benefit the action took place

LOCATION – the place at which an entity/action is situated

For each noun phrase (DP) in **bold type** in the following sentences, identify its theta-role. For the longer terms use the abbreviations **EXP**(IERENCER), **STIM**(ULUS), **INST**(RUMENT), **BEN**(EFICIARY), and **LOC**(ATION).

Max saw the comet (1) *Max:* .... *EXP* .... (2) *the comet:* .... *STIM* ....

We wrote a letter to Mary (3) *we:* .... (4) *a letter:* ....
(5) *to Mary:* ....

Jim chopped the wood with an axe (6) *Jim:* .... (7) *the wood:*
.... (8) *an axe:* ....

Make me a sandwich (9) *me:* .... (10) *a sandwich:* ....

They took from the rich and gave to the poor (11) *They:* .... (12)
the rich: .... (13) *the poor:* ....

(continued)

The Louvre is *in Paris*   (14) *The Louvre*: . . . .   (15) *Paris*: . . . .

Did you hear what I said?   (16) *you* . . . .   (17) *what I said*: . . . .

Kennedy died in *Dallas*   (18) *Kennedy*: . . . .   (19) *Dallas*: . . . .

Go from here to there   (20) *here*: . . . .   (21) *there*: . . . .

ASSIGNMENT 65* Subject Mapping

The θ-(theta-)roles borne by the DPs in the previous assignment were to be found in all parts of the sentence. Many of the DPs occurring within the VP (i.e. **internal arguments**) were complements/objects of prepositions: *in Paris, from here*, etc. A clue then as to the θ-role borne by a DP in the predicate is often a preposition of which the DP is a complement. Examples from the previous assignment:

> They took [*from the rich*] and gave [*to the poor*]
>   SOURCE   GOAL

> Jim chopped the wood [*with an axe*]
>   INST

> Kennedy died [*in Dallas*]
>   LOC

An internal argument DP adjacent to the verb – i.e. the **direct object** – is assigned case by the verb, not by a preposition, and its θ-role is thus not usually overtly marked. Again, examples from the previous assignment:

> Max saw [*the comet*]
>   STIM

> We wrote [*a letter*] to Mary
>   THEME

A DP occurring OUTSIDE the VP – that is, as subject – is the **external argument**. Whereas internal arguments are assigned their θ-roles by the verb, θ-role assignment for external arguments is by the VP. (For example, in order to determine that *Max* is agent in *Max threw the fight* but not in *Max threw a fit*, one must look not just at the verb *threw* but at the entire VP.) One of the striking characteristics of English is its relative freedom to map a variety of θ-roles onto its external arguments, or subjects. Further examples from the previous assignment:

(continued)

[Max] saw the comet
EXP

[Jim] chopped the wood with an axe
AGENT

[The Louvre] is in Paris
THEME

For each of the following examples, identify the θ-role that the **subject** represents, using the terms and abbreviations introduced in the previous assignment – i.e. AGENT, THEME, GOAL, SOURCE, EXP, STIM, INST, BEN, LOC. If no role is represented, write Ø.

1. *They've done us a favor* ......*AGENT*...

2. *We've been done a favor* ....

3. *Do **you** feel hot?* ....

4. *It's hot in here* ....

5. *The **key** opened the door* ....

6. ***Max** was given an award* ....

7. ***They** gave an award to Max* ....

8. *An **award** was given to Max* ....

9. *This **camper** sleeps six people* ....

10. *A **dollar** won't buy you much* ....

11. *The **boat** sank quickly* ....

12. *There's water on the floor* ....

13. ***Water's** on the floor* ....

14. *The **floor** has water on it* ....

15. *I'm freezing* ....

16. ***Somebody** broke my cup* ....

17. *My **cup** broke* ....

18. *My **guitar** broke a string* ....

19. *This **knife** won't cut the rope* ....

20. *This **knife** won't sharpen easily* ....

ASSIGNMENT 66** **Passive**

In the previous assignment appeared the following sentences:

> They gave an award to Max
> An award was given to Max
> Max was given an award

The verb *gave* in the first sentence is in the **active voice** and the verb *was given* in the second and third is in the **passive voice**. (See Assignment G for more focus on this voice distinction.) Although the propositional content is the same in all three, each has a different subject and each subject has a different θ-role – namely, *they* (agent), *an award* (theme), and *Max* (goal), respectively. Notice that notwithstanding the different positions of these three DPs vis-à-vis the verb, their thematic relationship to the verb remains constant. The underlying representations of the three sentences would therefore be something like the following:

(a)   [IP *They* [VP *gave an award to Max*]]

(b)   [IP e [VP *was given an award to Max*]]

(c)   [IP e [VP *was given Max an award*]]

   Although the verb *give* in any of its forms (*gave, was given*, etc.) will assign the appropriate θ-roles to its arguments, it will not assign objective case to its objects (*an award, Max*) unless it also has an external argument – i.e. subject. Passive verbs do not have subjects, subject position is thus empty in (b) and (c), and the passive verb *was given* therefore cannot case-mark its objects. Since *an award* in (b) and *Max* in (c) lack case they must move (i.e. **raise**) into subject position (Spec, IP), where they will be assigned nominative case by I (INFL). This forcing of NP (DP) movement in the derivation of the passive is one instance of what has been termed the **Extended Projection Principle (EPP)**, which can be stated simply as

A clause must have a subject

(continued)

179

A verb in the passive may of course also take a **clausal** complement:

(d) [$_{IP}$ e [$_{VP}$ *was believed* [$_{IP}$ **Max to merit an award**]]]
        Max was believed to merit an award

(e) [$_{IP}$ e [$_{VP}$ *was believed* [$_{CP}$ **that Max merited an award**]]]
        It was believed that Max merited an award

Again, since the passive *was believed* fails to θ-mark its subject, it cannot assign structural case to the clausal complement. *Max* must therefore move into subject position in (d). In (e), however, *Max* is assigned nominative case within the CP by a (finite) I (NFL) and therefore cannot move. The non-theta expletive or "dummy" element *it* must then fill subject position, in observance of the EPP.

Each of the ten sentences listed below is ungrammatical, the ungrammaticality identifiable by one or more of the factors cited here as (A) through (F). After each sentence write the letter(s) (A)–(F) corresponding to the following identifying factor(s):

(A) **failure of non-case assigned argument to move**
(B) **movement of wrong argument**
(C) **obligatory movement blocked by a filled subject position**
(D) **wrong base-generated position of external argument**
(E) **missing/wrong expletive**
(F) **passivized intransitive verb**

 1. **Was seen the accident by a lot of people*   . . . . .

 2. **It was seen the accident by a lot of people*   . . . . .

 3. **Saw the accident a lot of people*   . . . . .

 4. **A lot of people was seen the accident*   . . . . .

 5. **An accident was happened*   . . . . .

 6. **It was considered Max to have problems*   . . . . .

 7. **Was thought there to be a problem*   . . . . .

 8. **Was thought that there was a problem*   . . . . .

 9. **There was thought that it would be a problem*   . . . . .

10. **Were died a lot of animals*   . . . . .

ASSIGNMENT 67* Passive: L2

It was noted in the previous assignment that the passive-verb construction in English results from the interaction of two principles:

- **Passive morphology** prevents the verb from case-marking its DP object:

$$[_{IP} \text{ e } [_{VP} \textit{was written } [_{DP} \textit{the letter}]]]$$
$$[- \text{ case}]$$

- The **EPP** or **Extended Projection Principle** (i.e. that a clause must have a subject) forces the caseless DP to move/raise to subject position (i.e. Spec, IP), where it is assigned nominative case by INFL:

$$[_{IP} \textit{ The letter}_i [_{VP} \textit{was written } t_i]]$$

The passive is not the only construction, however, in which an otherwise caseless DP raises to subject position. Another example, encountered in Assignment 45, would be **raising verbs** such as *appear, happen, tend, have, fail*, etc.:

$$[_{DP} \textit{ The letter}_i] \textbf{ has } [_{IP} t_i \textit{ to be written}]$$

And closely related to **raising verbs** are the **raising adjectives** such as *certain, sure, likely*, etc.:

$$[_{DP} \textit{ The letter}_i] \textbf{ is likely } [_{IP} t_i \textit{ to be written}]$$

The final example is a type of intransitive verb termed **unaccusative**, such as *happen, exist, die, fall, disappear, arrive*, etc., whose sole (internal) DP argument bears the θ-role of **theme** (see assignments in Section B of this part for elaboration):

$$[_{IP} \textit{ The letter}_i [_{VP} \textbf{disappeared } t_i]]$$

(continued)

Research in L2 acquisition reveals many examples of production by learners with a variety of mother tongues in which an unaccusative verb has seemingly been "passivized":

> *After a week patient will **be died** [Japanese]
> *I **was** nearly **arrived** to my office [Italian]
> *The leaves **were fallen** down [Chinese]
> *Nobody would tell her what **was happened** [Spanish]
> *The cultural uniqueness **is** now **disappeared** [Korean]

A number of analyses of this construction have been offered in the L2 research literature, one of which, drawing on the syntax of all the **raising** constructions cited above, makes a great deal of sense. Note that of these four constructions in which a DP has moved or raised to subject position – namely, passive, raising verbs, raising adjectives, and unaccusatives – only the passive has a "marker," so to speak, of such movement: the *-ed* morphology of the past participle and the use of the copula *be*. What then might one plausibly (and simply) say the learner is doing in producing the above "passivized" unaccusatives?

ASSIGNMENT 68** Thematic Relations: L1
(data from Nishigauchi and Roeper 1987)

Consider the examples below of the structural uses of *for* in the speech of a child between the ages of 2 and 3½, where the three groups represent developmental stages. Note, for instance, the use of *for me* (*to blow on*) in example (b) and *for I* (*can put* ...) in example (f) and the ontological tendency to let new functions be expressed by old forms.

Stage I

(a) *I got some water for Lola to come back now*
     [= for the purpose of inducing the dog to return]
(b) *grandma has a present for me to blow on*
(c) *some berries for the birds to eat*
(d) *it's for the birds to eat*

Stage II

(e) *these are matches for make a fire*
(f) *this is for I can put some light on, so you won't be cold*
(g) *move it close for you can get in there*
(h) *I need some more for when my friends come back*
(i) *it's for fix things*
(j) *that's for wiping these off*
(k) *I want for you hold it* [*for you* is benefactive]
(l) *it's too big for you eat*

Stage III

(m) *let's bring a bench for to jump in*
(n) *I have a place for to put my girls, right here*
(o) *you can have a pocket for to put them in, Dad*
(p) *(what do you want to get in there for?) for to eat*
(q) *I can draw something, but I need a pencil for to*
(r) *this milk is for to drink*
(s) *these buttons are for to sew on you*
(t) *toys are for to play with*
(u) *vitamin C is for to grow*

(continued)

Briefly, how might each stage be characterized and what could all three be said to have in common, apart from the appearance of *for* itself?

ASSIGNMENT 69** Thematic Relations: L2 (data from Zobl 1984)

Consider the examples below of the structural uses of the word *for* in the speech of adult French-speaking learners of English in Canada:

(a)   *He needed money for to get a clean shirt*
(b)   *He goes to library for buy his book*
(c)   *How many oranges d'you want for buy?*
(d)   *He ask for do [= go] the movie*
(e)   *Phil decide on the street for speak again with the girl*
(f)   *My father encourage me for play hockey*
(g)   *He suggest for to shoot*
(h)   *He go for to meet the girl*

(i)   *And (they) is very happy for when he [= they] see the visitor*
(j)   *Phil come back for you [= Phil] give her the bill*
(k)   *He ask for his parents come to see him*
(l)   *The policeman stop the car for the people can cross the street*
(m)   *The young boy is not crying for because they have not good temperature outside?*

(n)   *She want to go for the disco*
(o)   *I would buy a trip for Florida*
(p)   *We went for Cincinnati*

(q)   *What is colour for taxi?*
(r)   *What is name for capital Saskatchewan?*
(s)   *Equilibrium for the nature is disturb*
(t)   *habits for the animals*
(u)   *mood for man*
(v)   *center for the note* [middle of the class; average]
(w)   *the next test for me Monday* [my next test ...]
(x)   *no car for me* [I don't have a car]
(y)   *It's a very beautiful performance for Minnesota North Stars*
(z)   *become a friend for her* [become her friend]
(aa) *parents for she* [her parents]

(continued)

What are the uses of *for*, as represented in the four different groups? Is it possible to tie any of these uses together into something more general? (Note that historically *for* at one time occurred before infinitives and also functioned as a directional preposition.) Finally, in what ways do these data with *for* resemble those of the L1 learner in the preceding assignment? In what ways are they different?

Learnability (Lexical Classes): L1

Theories of language learnability, however else they may differ conceptually, are based on the general assumption that learning takes place through the aid of positive evidence only (at least in childhood). A number of researchers – Pinker (1989) is a particularly good reference – have carried this assumption to research in the learning of pairs of verbs that are similar semantically but differ in the patterning of their argument structures: cf. the much-discussed *give/donate* example (*give some money to the charity / give the charity some money* vs. *donate some money to the charity / *donate the charity some money*). How, for instance is the child, once having made the *donate*-type error, able to expunge it without negative evidence? One solution among several that have been proposed (Randall 1992) makes use of (a) the nature of optionality and (b) presumed innate knowledge of the learner concerning the ordering of arguments:

(a)   Optionality of an argument is always learnable through positive evidence.

(b)   If an argument is optional, then it may not interpose between a head and an obligatory argument (Randall's **Order Principle**).

Thus, with respect to the *give/donate* examples, the **goal** argument (*the charity*) is **obligatory** for *give*, **optional** for *donate* (cf. *donate/*give some money*). All that is necessary for unlearning of the above ungrammatical *donate* example to take place is therefore the discovery, through positive evidence, of the optionality of its goal argument.

Examine now the following L1 data from Bowerman (1982) containing errors with *fill* and *spill*:

> *Can I fill some salt into the bear?
> *I don't want it because I spilled it of orange juice.

(continued)

Briefly, how would principles (a) and (b) work to eventually expunge these constructions from the child's grammar? You will find it helpful to compare the argument structures for *fill* and *spill* assumed here by the child with those of the adult grammar.

SECTION B Characteristics of the Verb

ASSIGNMENT 71** Intransitivity

One of the ways in which verbs have traditionally been classified is with respect to whether or not they take an object. Object-taking verbs are labeled **transitive**, as in *John hit Max*, whereas verbs taking no object are labeled **intransitive**, as in *John slept*. Verbs exhibiting surface characteristics of intransitivity, however, are a mixed bag and can be further distinguished syntactically and/or semantically:

(a) *John laughed/slept/talked*/etc.

(b) *John awakened/aged/changed*/etc.

(c) *John teases/bribes/angers easily.*
     (Cf. *You can tease/bribe/anger John easily.*)

(d) *John read/wrote/drove*/etc.
     (Cf. *read a book/wrote a letter/drove a car*)

Note then the following:

- In (a) *John* bears the θ-role **agent** and is himself the immediate causer of the event denoted by the verb.

- In (b) *John* bears the θ-role of **theme** and there is an implied (external) causer of the event denoted by the verb.

- In (c) *John* bears the θ-role of **theme** and an agent is implied.

- In (d) *John* bears the θ-role of **agent** and there is an understood NP object.

Verbs like those in (a) are called **unergative**, those in (b) **ergative**, those in (c) **middle**, and those in (d) **pseudo-transitive**. Diagnostics that can help to sort out these classifications are laid out below, where a starred parenthetical indicates that the item in parentheses is obligatory – for example:

*Ice keeps *(easily).*

(continued)

It is well to consider these as guidelines, however, rather than infallible heuristics:

	UNERGATIVE	ERGATIVE
resultative:	*John drank drunk	The ice froze solid
fake reflexive:	John drank himself drunk	*The ice froze itself solid
X's way:	John danced his way home	*The ice melted its way downstream
cognate object:	John slept a deep sleep	*The ice fell a smooth fall
causative alternation:	*Something shouted John (John shouted)	Something broke the ice (The ice broke)

	ERGATIVE	MIDDLE
genericness:	Yesterday the ice melted	*Yesterday the ice kept easily
progressive:	The ice is melting	*The ice is keeping easily
obligatory modification:	The ice melted (quickly)	Ice keeps *(easily)
preposing:	the melting ice	*the (easily) keeping ice
small clause:	I saw the ice melt	*I saw the ice keep (easily)

Note further the following:

- The seemingly intransitive middles are inherently transitive and thus always have a transitive counterpart.

- Ergatives are inherently transitive, where the transitive alternate expresses causation. That is, along with example (b) we may also have *Something awakened/aged/changed John.*

- Intransitives whose sole argument bears the θ-role of **theme**, such as **ergatives**, form part of a larger class of verbs that also includes **passives** (Assignment 66) and **raising verbs** (Assignment 45). The property that crgatives, passives, and raising verbs all have in common is that since they have no underlying subject to which to assign a θ-role, they cannot assign objective (accusative) case to their sole argument/theme. That is, we do not have *Awakened John*, *was awakened John*, *Seemed John to be awake*. The property in question has thus been termed **unaccusativity**.

- The underlying post-verbal position of the argument/theme for ergatives can be seen in the non-alternating subclass of these verbs termed **unaccusative** (Assignment 67), including verbs of **existence/appearance** and **spatial configuration**, and their occurrence in constructions with existential *there*:

> There **lived an old woman** in the house
> There **appeared a servant** at the door
> There **rested a ladder** against the wall
> There **stood a plant** in the corner

(continued)

Name: _____   Date: __ / __ / __   Class: _____

Using the above diagnostics to the extent possible, mark each of the following sentences with respect to the main verb (*italicized*) in the following way: "E" if it is ergative, "U" if it is unergative, "M" if it is middle, and "P" if it is pseudo-transitive. Some of the examples may be ambiguous. Note once more that ergatives may have transitive/intransitive alternation. Is there anything unusual about no. 15?

1. . . . Bach *transposes* more easily than Mozart.

2. . . . Bob *composes* more easily than Matt.

3. . . . Bob *reposes* more often than Matt.

4. . . . A person *decomposes* over a long period of time.

5. . . . This shirt *buttons* in back.

6. . . . This shirt *ripped* to shreds in the washer.

7. . . . My guitar *broke*.

8. . . . My guitar *cracked* open.

9. . . . My guitar *plays* well.

10. . . . John *plays* well. [ambiguous?]

11. . . . Will they *play* well in Peoria? [three ways ambiguous?]

12. . . . Watch the water *boil*.

13. . . . That's a good pot for *boiling* water.

14. . . . My wife *writes* better than my teacher.

15. . . . My pen *writes* better than my pencil.

16. . . . The jaguars *ran* themselves ragged.

17. . . . Jaguars *drive* well.

18. . . . They certainly *teach* a lot.

19. . . . They certainly *grow* a lot.

20. . . . They certainly *won* their way to fame.

21. . . . These controls don't *work*.

22. . . . These guys don't *work*. [ambiguous?]

ASSIGNMENT
72*
(In)transitivity

The lexical items in each of the lists below show properties that are reminiscent, in a very loose sense, of ergativity. For example, and X-*ee* in some cases is predicated (a) of someone who is X-*ed* and in others (b) of someone who X-*es*. Likewise, X-*able* in some cases is predicated (a) of someone or something that can be X-*ed* and in others (b) of someone or something that can X. Circle the words in each column that fit the (b) pattern and try to formulate a generalization for all these data in terms of (in)transitivity. Recall from the previous assignment that ergatives include a subclass (unaccusatives) that do not alternate.

1.	*trainee*	17.	*teachable*
2.	*employee*	18.	*perishable*
3.	*escapee*	19.	*washable*
4.	*payee*	20.	*likable*
5.	*nominee*	21.	*agreeable*
6.	*standee*	22.	*collapsible*
7.	*appointee*	23.	*winnable*
8.	*addressee*	24.	*answerable*
9.	*absentee*	25.	*comparable*
10.	*parolee*	26.	*workable*
11.	*devotee*		
12.	*draftee*		
13.	*divorcee*		
14.	*advisee*		
15.	*returnee*		
16.	*retiree*		

Name: _____   Date: __ / __ / __   Class: _____

ASSIGNMENT 73* Unaccusatives: L1

The underlying representation of **unaccusatives** (Assignment 67) is assumed to be the following (oversimplified) structure:

$$[_{IP}\ e\ [_{VP}\ V\ [DP]]]$$

Recall that unaccusatives lack a logical subject and that the sole argument is the logical object, bearing the **theme** relation. Again, unaccusatives are therefore similar in this respect to passives:

> $[_{IP}\ e\ [_{VP}\ was\ hidden\ [the\ letter]]]$ **passive**
> $[_{IP}\ e\ [_{VP}\ disappeared\ [the\ letter]]]$ **unaccusative**

The **Extended Projection Principle** (Assignment 66) requires that the theme argument be projected to subject position, yielding for these two examples:

> *The letter was hidden*
> *The letter disappeared*

Whether or not children at first have the means to accomplish such movement in their production has occasioned some amount of discussion in the acquisition research literature.

Listed in (a) are examples of English utterances produced by children around 2 years old, taken from Déprez and Pierce (1993):

(1) (a) *Going it*   (e) *Fall pants*
     (b) *Going (re)corder* (f) *Fall down lady*
     (c) *Come car*   (g) *Come Lois*
     (d) *Came a man*   (h) *Broken the light*

Compare the examples in (a) with others (b) of children of a similar age and culled from various sources:

(2) (i) *Daddy sleeping*   (m) *Baby sleep*
     (j) *Mommy eat*   (n) *Doggie bark*
     (k) *Mommy sit*   (o) *Mommy push*
     (l) *Daddy kick*   (p) *Doggie run*

(continued)

Consider now that few examples like those in (3), below, have yet been attested anywhere in the research literature:

(3) (q) *Sleeping daddy*   (u) *Sleep baby*
    (r) *Eat mommy*   (v) *Bark doggie*
    (s) *Sit mommy*   (w) *Push mommy* [agent]
    (t) *Kick daddy* [agent]   (x) *Run doggie*

In very general terms, how do the three groups differ and what factor(s) might account for the differences? Germane to this question is the fact that in English the base position of theme is to the right of the verb and of agent to the left of the verb.

ASSIGNMENT 74* Unaccusatives: L2 (I)
(data from Zobl 1989)

With reference to the facts of unaccusativity outlined in Assignments 71 and 73, consider commonly occurring examples of L2 English interlanguage such as the following:

(a) (i) *The most memorable experience of my life was happened 15 years ago* [Arabic/advanced]

(ii) *Most of people are fallen in love and marry with somebody* [Japanese/high intermediate]

(iii) *My mother was died when I was just a baby* [Thai/high intermediate]

(b) (i) *Sometimes comes a good regular wave* [Japanese/low intermediate]

(ii) *I was just patient until dried my clothes* [Japanese/high intermediate]

(iii) *After a few minutes arrive the girlfriend with his family* [Spanish/low intermediate]

(c) (i) *I think it continue of today condition forever* [Japanese/intermediate]

(ii) *It is so changing everything* [Japanese/?]

(iii) *It was nearly killed all of us* [Chinese/high intermediate]

Zobl (1989) claims that three separate but related learner strategies are at work here. Assuming that what the learners are reacting to in these verbs is the common lexical property of unaccusativity, consider briefly what three different strategies they could be resorting to in order to accommodate this property to requirements of UG and/or the grammar of English.

ASSIGNMENT   # Unaccusatives: L2 (II)
75*   (date from Rutherford 1989)

Examine the following two sets of (written) English IL data, the first (a)–(m) produced by L1 Spanish speakers, the second (n)–(v) by L1 Arabic speakers. Both groups exhibit wide proficiency ranges. Note in particular the constructions appearing in **bold type**.

L1 Spanish

(a)   *The education in G., **are changed** so much, because before, in the school for example, in any class many students, the study are not good ...*

(b)   *... but now **are a many telephones in each department** ...*

(c)   *On this particular place called G. ... **happened a story** which now appears on all Mexican history books, ...*

(d)   *The boy friend has to arrive to the church first and his family after a few minutes **arrive the girlfriend** with his family too*

(e)   *I have mentioned that in my country **does not appear to exist any constraint on a woman's right** to choose a husband*

(f)   *And then at last **comes the great day***

(g)   *In the town **lived a small Indian**, ...*

(h)   *Then **began the wars** to reconquer the land*

(i)   *In my country **is very easy** to choose a husband or wife because the fathers of the man or woman not participe in this choose*

(j)   *In my country I often visited the caribean island near to my city, now **is impossible for me** to go there*

(k)   *Second **is necessary** that all youngs in my country to know very well others cultures*

(l)   *In the lake of Maracaibo **was discovered the oil***

(m)   *In this one **was placed the national school of engineering***

(continued)

L1 Arabic

(n) *... but lately **happen some extra things** or little changes on this custom because of the civilization*

(o) *After that, they'll be lead to their house, and with that **comes the end of the wedding***

(p) *The first people to come into the church were the closest relatives of the bride and bridegroom and then **came the rest of the invited people***

(q) *The bride was very attractive, on her face **appeared those two red cheeks** and above them beautiful deep eyes*

(r) *On the walls of this monument **are written the names of the victories of Napoleon's battles***

(s) *Also **it is important the right person** who want to be one of the staff*

(t) *Really, **it is terrible the situation in Lebanon***

(u) *... after that they lock for the age. because **must be the age similar for bowth or neerly***

(v) *Now we are going to the "arc de Triomphe" where **lies the thumb of the unknown soldier***

With reference to the matter of unaccusatives (Assignment 73) and the three strategies revealed in IL unaccusativity in the previous assignment, what observations would you want to make concerning these two sets of IL data? Are there any VS constructions in these data that are GRAMMATICAL in English?

Name: _____   Date: __ / __ / __   Class: _____

ASSIGNMENT 76** Unaccusatives: L2 (III)

What we have been referring to as unaccusativity is a widely documented linguistic phenomenon. However, whereas its **semantic** features have some cross-linguistic consistency, unaccusatives do not necessarily reveal **syntactic** characteristics from one language to another. Moreover, languages that do show such syntactic reflexes usually differ in terms of both the kind and the extent of the reflex. In the Romance languages, for instance, the syntactic unaccusative feature of AUX selection (the form of the auxiliary used in perfect aspect) – namely, *be* over *have* – has different ranges of occurrence: for example, Italian consistently selects *essere* ("be") over *avere* ("have"), whereas French selection of *être* over *avoir* is very limited. (Note that English, with its exclusive selection of *have*, makes no such distinction at all.) Furthermore, preference for "be" among native speakers of Italian ranges over a semantic hierarchy (from **core** to **peripheral** unaccusatives) and historical bleaching out in French of "be" in favor of "have" has proceeded in terms of that hierarchy as well.

What then might happen in a language contact situation involving native speakers of these three languages? Sorace (1993) looked at the acquisition of L2 Italian by native speakers of French and of English who were judged to have near-native fluency in Italian. The subjects were asked to judge the grammaticality of Italian sentences representing three properties of unaccusativity, including the above AUX-selection property. Her results showed (a) that both the French and English subjects were sensitive to the unaccusative semantics of the hierarchy, but (b) that the intuitions of both groups of learners, though they were extremely advanced, differed noticeably from those of native Italians. Specifically, one group showed **determinate** intuitions (i.e. definite but divergent vis-à-vis native Italians), whereas the other group showed ɪɴ**determinate** intuitions (i.e. random and incomplete vis-à-vis native Italians). With nothing else to go on here, which learner group (English or French) would you guess had the divergent intuitions and which the incomplete – and (briefly) why?

SECTION C Tense, Aspect, Modality

Name: _____ Date: __ / __ / __ Class: _____

Contrasts in Tense/
Mode/Aspect/Voice (I)

Traditional grammarians have noted that the English **predicate phrase** (I-bar in generative terms) can manifest a number of contrasts; that is,

- contrast in **tense**: [**past** / present]
  wrote / *write*

- contrast in **mode**: [**modal** / non-modal]
  may write / *write*

- contrast in **aspect** (**perfect**): [**perfect** / non-perfect]
  have written / *write*

- contrast in **aspect** (**progressive**): [**progressive** / non-progressive]
  be writing / *write*

- contrast in **voice** [**passive** / active]
  be written / *write*

With reference to these distinctions, identify the number of contrasts evident in each of the following pairs and state the contrasting properties in question:

1. *is ill / was ill*   *1. present/past* . . . .

2. *was ill / has been ill*   . . . .

3. *is going / may be going*   . . . .

4. *is going / may have been going* . . . .

5. *knows / has known*   . . . .

6. *knew / was known*   . . . .

7. *saw / was being seen*   . . . .

8. *must see / must have seen*   . . . .

9. *is leaving / must have left*   . . . .

10. *has talked about / is being*   . . . .
       talked about

ASSIGNMENT 78*   Contrasts in Tense/ Mode/Aspect/Voice (II)

With reference to the distinctions in **tense, mode, aspect,** and **voice** that can be rendered by VP/I′, as in the previous assignment, complete each verb phrase below to illustrate the SETS of contrasting properties (and only those properties) indicated. Take the "DP verb / verb DP" citation as being UNMARKED for all five properties listed. In other words, load all the designated properties onto the written out portion for each example.

1. active/passive; perfect/non-perfect
    write DP: *DP has been written* . . . .

2. modal/non-modal; progressive/non-progressive
    DP *drive:* . . . .

3. present/past; active/passive; perfect/non-perfect
    see DP: . . . .

4. modal/non-modal; active/passive
    move DP: . . . .

5. present/past; progressive/non-progressive; perfect/non-perfect
    DP *think:* . . . .

6. modal/non-modal;   active/passive;   progressive/non-progressive;   perfect/ non-perfect
    beat DP: . . . .

Name: _____   Date: __ / __ / __   Class: _____

ASSIGNMENT 79* Modality: Deontic vs. Epistemic

The English modals are traditionally identified as *will, would, can, could, must, may, might, shall, should,* and possibly *need* and *dare* as well. Although a number of non-modals (e.g. *have to, be allowed to,* etc.) have rough semantic equivalents among the modals proper, only the latter can serve as lexical heads (I) of INFL and therefore undergo movement to C(omp) to produce interrogative constructions.

It is also traditional to draw a semantic distinction for a given modal as between two senses: **deontic** (from the Greek *deon(t)* "that which is binding or needful") and **epistemic** (from the Greek *episteme* "knowledge, understanding"). In deontic (sometimes called "root") modality, the speaker expresses obligation, permission, or ability to engage in a certain action: "You must leave now;" "You may leave now." In epistemic modality, the speaker expresses "possibility or necessity ... modulated for commitment and evidence" (Frawley 1992: 408): "You must be kidding;" "You may be right." Most of the modals listed above can each encode these two senses, often ambiguously: "They should be here" (i.e. "it is incumbent upon them to be here" vs. "it's a good guess that they're here"). It is well to recognize, however, that the semantics of modality is more complex than it is possible to convey in a work of this kind, a useful reference being Quirk et al. (1985).

(continued)

For the modal in each of the following sentences, write D if you think it is deontic, E if epistemic.

1.   ... *He* CAN'T *be here* ...   [I don't believe it!]

2.   ... *He should be here* ...   [He has an obligation]

3.   ... *He wouldn't be here* ...   [... even if you paid him]

4.   ... *He could be here* ...   [It's very possible]

5.   ... *He won't be here* ...   [He's sick]

6.   ... *He could be here* ...   [... if he wanted to]

7.   ... *He must be here* ...   [It's an order]

8.   ... *He won't be here* ...   [He refuses]

9.   ... *He must be here* ...   [There's his hat]

10.   ... *He may be here* ...   [He has permission]

11.   ... *He should be here* ...   [He doesn't live far]

12.   ... *He may be here* ...   [That's my guess]

13.   ... *He wouldn't be here* ...   [... if he were sick]

14.   ... *He can be here* ...   [No reason to think not]

15.   ... *He can't be here* ...   [His car broke down]

16.   ... *He can be here* ...   [Nothing prevents him]

17.   ... *He* COULDN'T *be here* ...   [He's on a flight to Cairo]

18.   ... *He couldn't be here* ...   [He told me that over the phone]

19.   ... *He must not be here* ...   [I don't see him anywhere]

20.   ... *He mustn't be here* ...   [It would spoil everything]

ASSIGNMENT 80* Modality: L1/L2

Recall from the previous assignment that most of the English modal auxiliaries can encode both the **deontic** and the **epistemic** sense. Consider now in what ways these two senses might be acquired in the actual learning situations for children (L1) and for adults (L2). Given the general tendency in acquisition to assign one form to one meaning in the earliest stages, we will assume (as the research literature seems to indicate) that the deontic and epistemic senses of individual modals will not be acquired simultaneously, in L1 or L2. In these circumstances it appears that there are two possible ways in which acquisition of full target modality can proceed:

(a)   **a given modal will be acquired first for only one of its two senses, the other sense added later;**

(b)   **both senses will be acquired at around roughly the same time, but one will be encoded in a true modal, the other in a non-modal (periphrastic) expression of some kind** (e.g. sentence-external *maybe* for *may*, *be supposed to* for *should*, etc.).

One of these procedures (a) or (b) generally characterizes acquisition of modality in childhood, the other in adulthood. Documented examples of early L1 use of modality, with *can* and *will* being the first to appear, are typically ones like *I can make a big one / Can you help me?* (Foster 1990) and *Where the other Joe will drive? / Will you help me?* (Radford 1994). On the basis of such considerations as the learner's cognitive (im)maturity, language-learning history, social needs, etc., and of the degree of cognitive complexity (NOT linguistic complexity!) encoded in the deontic/epistemic sense of the modal, which of the two procedures would you guess is characteristic of which acquisition event (L1/L2) and why?

ASSIGNMENT 81*

Tense/Aspect: L2 (I)
(data from Wenzell 1989)

A distinction is traditionally drawn in aspectual terms between action viewed as complete or **perfective** and action viewed as incomplete or **imperfective** (Quirk et al. 1985). In English, the canonical realization of perfective aspect is the **simple past**; the canonical realization of the imperfective is the **progressive** (present and past), as exemplified in Assignment 77. Related to the perfective/imperfective distinction is one of **foreground** vs. **background**. As stated by Bardovi-Harlig (1994: 43):

> The foreground relates events belonging to the skeletal structure of the discourse ... and consists of clauses that move time forward ... The background does not itself narrate main events, but provides supportive material that elaborates on or evaluates the events in the foreground.

With these distinctions in mind, examine the English L2 data below produced by a middle-aged native Russian speaker after more than two years in the United States but with limited exposure to English.

(a) *How do I meet my husband?*
He, he live too in Odessa all all.
An I live in Odessa.
An he work.
I all day I take the bus in the institute.
An he work near.
In the same bus I we go.

[How did I meet my husband?
He also lived in Odessa all his life.
And I lived in Odessa.
And he was working there.
Every day I would take the bus to the institute.
And he worked near there.
We would go on the same bus.]

(continued)

(b) *And then I, I met my husband in ninety forty-six.*
    I was an I married in July, in July I was married.
    February 7, ninety forty-seven, February.
    An in I ended institute
    February I ended institute.

    [And then I met my husband in 1946.
    And I married in July, in July I was married.
    February 7, 1947, February.
    I finished [my studies] at the institute.
    In February I finished at the institute.]

Briefly, what observation might be made from a discourse perspective concerning the use of present and past FORMS of the verb?

ASSIGNMENT 82* Tense/Aspect: L2 (II)
(data from Kumpf 1984)

Keeping in mind the observations you made in the previous assignment, examine the following English interlanguage data produced by a native Japanese
speaker (Tomiko) after 28 years of residence in the United States. Clauses that
are italicized are identified as foregounded from a discourse perspective. What
observation could be made concerning the presence/absence here of past-tense
FORM?

First time Tampa have a tornado come to.
Was about seven forty-five.
Bob go to work,
n I was inna bathroom
5 *and ... a ... tornado come*
shake everything.
Door was flyin open,
I was scared.
Hanna was sittin in window ...
10 Hanna is a little dog.
French poodle.
I call Baby.
Anyway, she never wet bed,
she never wet anywhere.
15 But she was so scared
an cryin,
run to the bathroom,
cometo me,
an she tinkle, tinkle, tinkle all over me. [laugh]
20 She was so scared
I see somebody throwin a brick onna trailer
wind was blowin so hard
ana light ... outside street light was on
oh I was really scared.

(continued)

217

25 *An den second stop* ["and then in a second it stopped"]
    So I try to open door
    I could not open
    I say, "Oh my God. What's happen?"
    I look window / / awning was gone.

ASSIGNMENT **Present Perfect: L2**
83*

Aspect in English shows two forms, one for **progressive** and the other for **perfect**. The English perfect, in the words of Comrie (1976: 52), "indicates the continuing present relevance of a past situation," as in *I've now started Swahili lessons.* Comrie (1976: ch. 3) further identifies four particular instantiations of this more general property:

(a) **result/state:** ("a present state is referred to as being the result of some past situation")
     e.g. *John has arrived*

(b) **experiential:** ("a given situation has held at least once during some time in the past leading up to the present")
     e.g. *Bill has been to America*

(c) **persistent situation:** ("a situation ... started in the past but continues (persists) into the present")
     e.g. *I've shopped there for years*

(d) **recent past:** ("the present relevance of the situation referred to is simply one of temporal closeness")
     e.g. *They've just called*

The development of perfect aspect in L2 English acquisition was examined in a study by K. Flynn (1985). Flynn found that although learner production initially revealed the core **present relevance / past situation** characteristic of the perfect, subsequent interlanguage development of the four peripheral senses tended to follow native language lines. That is, where an above particular property happened to be encoded in the native language, that property tended to surface as a manifestation of the perfect in the English IL before an L1 property that was not coded.

Listed below are examples drawn from the three IL samples (one each for Mandarin, Arabic, and Spanish) of Flynn's corpus, with the developing perfect forms in question in **bold type**. Try to identify each in terms of the four specific properties listed above, using the labels **R/S** for **result/state**, **Exp** for **experiential**, **PS** for **persistent situation**, and **RP** for **recent past**. Nos. 1 through 8 are from the Chinese data, 9 through 14 from the Arabic data, and 15 through 20 from the Spanish data.

(continued)

Name: _____   Date: __ / __ / __   Class: _____

1. . . . . *However, the role **have been changes** in past decade*

2. . . . . *Since then, through many ways, we **work** hard to built up our economy*

3. . . . . *The Gross National Product **has raised** double and double*

4. . . . . *From time to time, till now, women in our country **has** the same position as men*

5. . . . . *Because I **have left** my country for years, . . .*

6. . . . . *. . . and the women **has been** a neglected part for a long time*

7. . . . . *In recent years, the general idea **is changed** largely*

8. . . . . *. . . you will be surprised to find that women **have walk** out of the kitchen*

9. . . . . *In a few years ago the role **has been changed***

10. . . . . *Since S.A. foundation in 1932, it **has been flowing** the reloguos law in everything*

11. . . . . *In the recent years the women in my country **start to have** the rights in almost everything*

12. . . . . *However, some people thinks that the role of women **has gone** far and we should stop it*

13. . . . . *Finally, there **are** many things **changed** in recent years*

14. . . . . *. . . and because of these limited rules, women **have become occupied** many important jobs*

15. . . . . *I have tremendous responsability now. **I'm finish** to my responsability to my family*

16. . . . . *They **have had** a lot of bussines days since they planned to get married*

17. . . . . *Never I **go** thee before*

18. . . . . *Now that this essential basis **has been set**, . . .*

19. . . . . *The women **has become** an important part in our political and social community . . .*

20. . . . . *First, they [women] dedicated the domestic works, but in recent years **have been** a progressive changes*

ASSIGNMENT 84** **Lexical Aspect**

The kind of **aspect** figuring so far in the material of this section was first displayed in Assignment 77, whose examples are repeated here:

- **aspect (perfect):**   [**perfect** / non-perfect]
                *have **written** / write*

- **aspect (progressive):** [**progressive** / non-progressive]
                *be **writing** / write*

Perfect and **progressive** constitute the two subcategories in English of what has been termed **grammatical aspect,** in that it is expressed by means of the GRAM-MATICAL markers of the auxiliary *have* for the perfect and *be* for the progressive. Grammatical aspect "reflects the way in which the verb action is *regarded* or *experienced* with respect to time" (Quirk et al. 1985: 188).

Aspectual characteristics are also inherent in verbs themselves – more properly, in entire verb phrases or predicates – hence the term **lexical aspect,** which is "independent of any grammatical marking or time frame. Put another way, lexical aspect resides in the 'sense' of a predicate, not in its 'reference'" (Robison 1995: 346).

Lexical aspect is divided by Vendler (1967) into four categories, labeled as follows, where the descriptions here can be at best only approximations:

- **state** (involuntary situation requiring no expenditure of energy; conditions, properties, habits, relations)
  e.g. *know, believe, love, possess, want, (dis)like, hate,* etc.

- **activity** (constant expenditure of energy and no definite completion)
  e.g. *run, walk, pull, talk, eat, write, swim, smoke,* etc.

- **accomplishment** (situation has duration and reaches completion)
  e.g. *paint a picture, make a chair, build a house, teach a class, play a game, read a book,* etc.

- **achievement** (completion perceived as being reached instantly)
  e.g. *reach the top, win the race, realize, recognize, lose/find something, cross the street, start, stop,* etc.

(continued)

Name: _____   Date: __ / __ / __   Class: _____

Therefore, notice contrasts such as the following:

[activity]	She *ran*
[accomplishment]	She *ran a mile*
[state]	We ***thought that*** he succeeded
[activity]	We ***thought about*** his success
[state]	They'*re married*
[achievement]	They *got married*
[accomplishment]	I *delivered a sermon*
[achievement]	I *delivered a pizza*

Although it is not always clear as to which of these four categories of lexical aspect a given verb or predicate will enter, there are a few diagnostics that can provide some help. For each of the diagnostics listed below, indicate with an "x" which of the four aspect categories – **state/activity/accomplishment/achievement** – you think the diagnostic serves to single out as grammatical (in most cases more than one) and provide a few verbs, VPs, or predicates as examples:

	STATE	ACTIVITY	ACCOMPLISH- MENT	ACHIEVE- MENT
• suffixation with *-ing* e.g.	. . .	. . .	. . .	. . .
• *How long did you* . . . .? e.g.	. . .	. . .	. . .	. . .
• *How long did you take to* . . . .?	. . .	. . .	. . .	. . .
e.g.				
• *At what time did you* . . . .? e.g.	. . .	. . .	. . .	. . .
• *You started to* . . . . e.g.	. . .	. . .	. . .	. . .

ASSIGNMENT 85** Lexical Aspect: L2

Presented in Assignment 81 were data from Wenzell (1989), reproduced below, concerning the use of present- and past-tense morphology in the production of an adult learner of English with limited proficiency:

(a) *How do I **meet** my husband?*
     *He, he **live** too in Odessa all all.*
     *An I **live** in Odessa.*
     *An he **work**.*
     *I all day I **take** the bus in the institute.*
     *An he **work** near.*
     *In the same bus I we **go**.*

(b) *And then I, I **met** my husband in ninety forty-six.*
     *I was an I **married** in July, in July I was **married**.*
     February 7, ninety forty-seven, February.
     *An in I **ended** institute*
     *February I **ended** institute.*

It was noted that the contrasting verb morphology – **present** in the first set, **past** in the second – correlated not with **tense** (since both sets are concerned with what happened in past time) but with the notions of **background** and **fore-ground,** respectively.

It has also been claimed by a number of acquisition researchers that mor-phological marking such as English *-ed* and *-s* is first used to mark aspectual features, and only later to mark tense. From this perspective, one could say that in the above data the aspectual uses of *-ed* in the second set represent the **perfective** and the (uninflected) root form in the first represents the **imperfective.** These would constitute examples of learner deployment of **grammatical aspect,** as mentioned in the previous assignment.

Is there anything to be noted as well of **lexical aspect** with reference to the verbs themselves (in **bold type**)? In terms of the Vendler categories from the previous assignment, *live, work, take the bus,* and *go* from the background set would all be classified as **activity** (the initial occurrence of *meet* is presumably a repetition of the interlocutor's question) and *met, (was) married,* and *ended*

(continued)

from the foreground set would all be **achievement**. Another way to depict this contrast would be to say that *met, (was) married,* and *ended* all involve events perceived as instantaneous, or **punctual** events, whereas *live, work, take the bus,* and *go* all involve duration, or **durative** events.

Punctual/durative is one of three basic semantic distinctions proposed by Comrie (1976) for lexical aspect. The other two are **stative/dynamic** and **telic/ atelic**. In the simplest terms, stative/dynamic has to do with whether or not the output of energy plays a part: yes for dynamic, no for stative. The telic/atelic distinction has to do with whether or not the predicate embodies a well-defined endpoint: yes for telic, no for atelic. Although these three binary distinctions for lexical aspect are thus somewhat more fine-grained than the four Vendler categories, the former can be systematically mapped onto the latter, as Andersen (1991) has done, where the arrows are intended to capture the scope of the feature in question:

STATE	:	ACTIVITY	:	ACCOMPLISHMENT	:	ACHIEVEMENT
← stative	:	dynamic ―――――――――――――――――――――――――――――――――――――→
←――――――――――― atelic	:	telic ―――――――――――――――→
←―――――――――――――――――――― durative	:	punctual ―――→

Consider again the adult language learner's task in acquiring English tense and aspect. We have already noted the claim that L2 interlanguage verb morphology will serve initially to denote aspect rather than tense. Given the above Wenzell data produced by a learner of low proficiency, and the Comrie semantic distinctions for lexical aspect, it is possible to plot the path that learners will take in moving from no verbal inflection to final use of *-ed* to designate **past**. Such a path can be represented by means of a schema devised by Andersen (1991: 318), where representative (irregular) verb tokens are supplied but the relevant features from the **stative/dynamic – telic/atelic – durative/punctual** distinctions need to be added:

0	→	. . . .	→	. . . .	→	. . . .	→	Past
no verbs inflected		*left*		*left* *taught*		*left* *taught* *ran*		*left* *taught* *ran* *had*

Write in the appropriate semantic feature, one from each of the three contrasts, whose scope captures those of the verb(s) exemplified.

ASSIGNMENT # Aspect vs.
86** Discourse: L2

Observe once more that analysis of the L2 acquisition data from Wenzell (1989) originally presented in Assignment 81 has taken two different routes. In that original assignment, the distribution in the data of present and past forms of the verb was given an accounting based upon the **discourse** notions of **foreground** and **background**, where linguistic aspect did not figure prominently. In the previous assignment those same data were given an accounting based upon features of linguistic **aspect** derived from models proposed by Vendler and by Comrie. In fact, these two approaches have come to represent the two prevailing hypotheses concerning L2 learner early deployment of verb morphology:

- The **aspect hypothesis** states that "target language verbal morphemes, independent of their function in the target language, are first used by the learner to mark aspect" (Robison 1990: 316).

- The **discourse hypothesis** states that "learners use emerging verbal morphology to distinguish foreground from background in narratives" (Bardovi-Harlig 1994: 43).

Deciding on what might constitute evidence in support of one or the other hypothesis is not an easy matter. Some of the factors that would need to be considered are the kinds of datum that have been collected (longitudinal vs. cross-sectional, oral vs. written), the number of subjects involved, their proficiency level, their native language, whether or not their learning is via formal instruction, etc. Crucial, however, is the matter of what exactly to look for, since for certain kinds of datum the two hypotheses will make the same prediction. With reference once more to the data from Wenzell (1989) displayed in Assignment 81, note that from the aspectual side the broadest contrast would be between **telic** and **atelic**. Initial deployment of past tense morphology is therefore predicted by the Aspect Hypothesis to occur with telic verbs and by the Discourse Hypothesis to occur with foregrounded verbs. Likewise, LACK of tense morphology would be predicted for atelic verbs by the Aspect Hypothesis, backgrounded verbs by the Discourse Hypothesis. If research bears out these predictions, then BOTH hypotheses are supported.

(continued)

Very simply then, what kinds of datum would serve to support (1) the Aspect Hypothesis but not the Discourse Hypothesis and (2) the Discourse Hypothesis but not the Aspect Hypothesis?

ASSIGNMENT	**Aspect: Dialect**
87*	(data from Wolfram and Christian 1980)

In a dialect of English spoken in the Appalachian Mountains, one hears sentences like the following:

> *I knew he was **a-telling** the truth, but still I was **a-coming** home.*
> *... and he says "Who's **a-stomping** on my bridge?"*
> *... and John boy, he come **a-running** out there and got shot.*
> *He just kept **a-begging** and **a-crying** and **a-wanting** to go out.*

Also observed in that region is an apparently common bumper-sticker message which reads:

> *If You See This Van **A-Rockin'**, Don't Come **A-Knockin'***

Note that one does NOT hear, or see, sentences like the following, which have been judged to be ungrammatical in this dialect:

> **The **a-running** was fun*
> **He enjoyed **a-swimming***
> **He died from **a-working** so hard*

Nor does one hear sentences like the following:

> **She's very **a-charming***
> **She's an **a-charming** person*

Very briefly (one sentence!), what is the rule in Appalachian English for prefixation with *a-*?

. . . .

. . . .

SECTION D Reference and Anaphora

ASSIGNMENT 88* Pro-Forms: N′

Laid out in Assignment 7 was the basic "template" for phrase-structure representation termed **X-bar** or **X′**, a configuration accommodating **heads, complements, adjuncts, specifiers,** and **maximal projections.** Heads and their maximal projections are the only labeled nodes in X′ theory that MUST be present in any such configuration and are symbolized in the template as "X" and "XP," respectively:

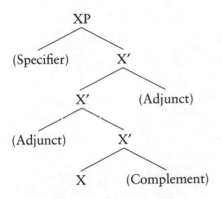

The configuration displayed below is designed to represent the structure of the DP *the phrase on this page.* Provide the CATEGORY label (note: not the above FUNCTIONAL label) for each box within the DP. Then write the actual words under the five lexical heads.

(continued)

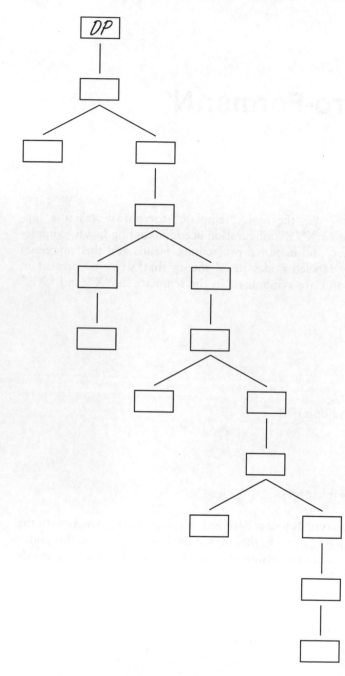

Number the three N′ constituents, with no. 1 being the highest and no. 3 the lowest; which of the three would represent the word *one* in the phrase "the *one* on this page"?

No. . . .

ASSIGNMENT **Pro-Forms:**
89*   **DP, NP**

The following tree represents a particular construction displaying both **definite-ness** and **specific indefiniteness** (see Assignment 8):

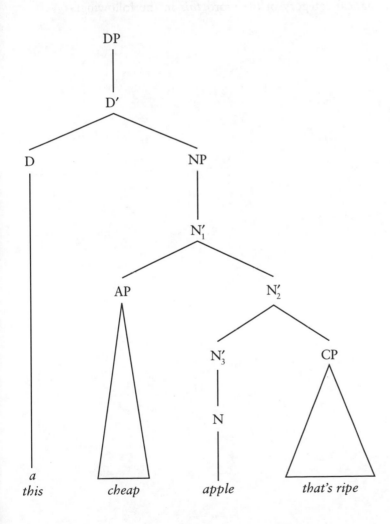

a
this   cheap   apple   that's ripe

(continued)

With reference to the tree, indicate what pro-form – i.e. pro-DP, pro-NP, pro-N′ – the word *one* represents in each of the following phrases in **bold type** and write out its antecedent:

1. *I don't want that expensive apple that's ripe; I want **this cheap one***
    pro-..... ....

2. *He saw a cheap apple that's ripe, and I saw **one** too*
    pro-..... ....

3. *I don't want that apple; I want this cheap **one** that's ripe*
    pro-..... ....

4. *I don't want* THAT *cheap apple that's ripe; I want **this one***
    pro-..... ....

What is the grammatical category of the word *this* in the following:

5. *I want **this***
    category: .....

ASSIGNMENT 90* Pro-Forms: Various

For each of the following examples, identify the underlined pro-constituent and write out its antecedent. Keep in mind the distinction drawn in the previous assignment between specific and non-specific indefinites. Sketching the tree for the clause containing the pro-form can often facilitate the identification.

For example:

> If that assignment was too easy, then this **one** is too.
> pro-*NP*   *assignment* . . . .

1. Some of the students were apprehensive about syntax at the beginning of the semester but less **so** at the end.
   pro-. . . . .

2. They said they would leave in the morning and we said we would **do so** as well.
   pro-. . . . .

3. She's looking for a better solution and I'm looking for **one** too.
   pro-. . . . .

4. They saw the aurora borealis and we saw **it** too.
   pro-. . . . .

5. Run away? Is that what they **did**?
   pro-. . . . .

6. A: You're not interested in what I'm saying. B: I am **so**!
   pro-. . . . .

7. A: Are they coming? B: I think **so**.
   pro-. . . . .

ASSIGNMENT **Pro-Form**
91* **vs. Ellipsis**

Most of the following forms in **bold type** are **pro-constituents,** whereas a few
stand for the remainder of a constituent in which **ellipsis** (of something following) has occurred. Identify each form as one or the other and then write out the
antecedent for the pro-constituent or the absent material via ellipsis.

1. *Has the news reached home yet? I'm afraid* **so.**
   pro-CP   (that) the news has reached home . . . .

2. *They liked the sentence as it was, so I left that word* **in.**
   . . . .

3. *Sally likes movies with action but Sue likes* **ones** *with talking.*
   . . . .

4. *I'd like some more coffee if you have* **any.**
   . . . .

5. *John didn't take it, but clearly* SOMEBODY **did.**
   . . . .

6. *John says no one took it, but clearly somebody* DID.
   . . . .

7. *John got a first prize this year and I got* **one** *last year.*
   . . . .

8. *All five escaped,* **which** *couldn't have been very easy.*
   . . . .

9. *If you look for a possible route to take, you'll surely find* **one.**
   . . . .

10. *If you don't study for the exam you'll regret* **it.**
    . . . .

ASSIGNMENT 92* Pronouns, Anaphors, and Pro-Constituents

Referential words, or words that refer to something else in the sentence or discourse, assume a variety of forms. Moreover, the "something else" ranges over everything from nouns to sentences. Some of this has been encountered in previous assignments. For convenience, we may divide them into **pronouns**, **anaphors**, and **pro-constituents**. Of the three, "pronoun" has broad interpretation and is typically a cover term as well for the wh- words used in questions and relative clauses.

The **pronouns** are thus usually cited as follows:

- **indefinite** (*any-/some-/every-/no- -one/-body*)

- **interrogative** (*who(m), whose, what, which, where, when, why, how*)

- **relative** (*who(m), whose, which, where, when, why*)

- **demonstrative** (*this, that, these, those*)

- **personal** (*I/me, you, he/him, she/her, we/us, they/them*)

- **possessive** (*my/mine, your/yours, his, her/hers, our/ours, their/theirs*)

The first- and second-person **personal** and **possessive** "pronouns" are not really "pro-" anything; they are actually **determiners**, as are the **demonstratives**.

Anaphors always have an antecedent within the clause or phrase that contains them and are of two types:

- **reflexive** (all the forms containing the suffixes *-self/-selves*)

- **reciprocal** (*each other, one another*)

The **pro-constituents**, as seen in Assignment 90, substitute for a variety of grammatical categories:

- **pro-DP** (*A teacher?*) *Yes; I saw* **one**

- **pro-NP** (*That tall teacher?*) *Yes; I saw that* **one**

(continued)

Name: _____ Date: __ / __ / __ Class: _____

- pro-N' (*Which one?*) *The **one** who teaches music*
- pro-I' (*He **ran away***) *That's what he **did***
- pro-VP (*Did he **run away?***) *Did he really **do so?***
- pro-AP (*She's not **very interested***) *She is **so**!*
- pro-CP (*Did he **leave?***) *I don't think **so***

Identify the **pronouns, anaphors,** and **pro-constituents** in **bold type** as one or another of the above referential types. For the pro-constituents, cite the subcategory – e.g. pro-VP, pro-N', etc.

1. *reciprocal* . . . . *The two sisters married **each other**'s brother*

2. *pro-CP* . . . . *Some say the world is flat, but I don't believe **it***

3. . . . . *We're creating problems for ourselves, that's what we're **doing***

4. . . . . *Who's the guy **whose** shirt's on backwards?*

5. . . . . *Is there **anyone** here who speaks Serbo-Croatian?*

6. . . . . ***Where**'s Sally?*

7. . . . . *Where's Sally? **She**'s outside*

8. . . . . *Some say it's you who took the money, but I think Fred's the **one***

9. . . . . *Some say it's you who took the money, but I think Fred's the **one** who took it*

10. . . . . *Some say Fred's a thief, but Bob's **one** too*

11. . . . . ***He** who loves himself loves everyone*

12. . . . . *He **who** loves himself loves everyone*

13. . . . . *He who loves **himself** loves everyone*

14. . . . . *He who loves himself loves **everyone***

15. . . . . *Does she throw it away? Is that what she **does**?*

16. . . . . *Is she throwing it away? Is that what she's **doing**?*

17. . . . . *Did **you** throw it away? Is that what **you** did?*

18. . . . . *Does it reach 90 mph? Is it **that** fast?*

19. . . . . *Does it reach 90 mph? Is it as fast as **that**?*

20. . . . . *Does that little car reach 90 mph? Is **it** that fast?*

ASSIGNMENT 93* Forward and Backward Pronominalization: L1

The following sentence types were used by Lust (1981) to elicit imitation by children of sentences containing possible combinations of two intersecting syntactic features:

- **main clause / subordinate clause** (in either order)

- **NP / repeated NP**, and **NP / (coreferential) pronoun** (each in either order)

The actual sentence types containing these phenomena used by Lust are the following (1981: 78), where the subscript "s" specifies subordinate clause:

NP / NP

(a) **NP - NP$_s$**
   Jane was sad, because Jane dropped the ice cream cone.
   Mary was sad while Mary was playing ball.

(b) **NP$_s$ - NP**
   Because Sam was thirsty, Sam drank some soda.
   While Dad was driving the car, Dad bumped a truck.

NP / Pronoun

(c) **NP - Pro$_s$**
   Tommy ran fast because he heard a lion.
   Jenna drank some juice while she was having lunch.

(d) **Pro$_s$ - NP**
   Because she was tired, Mommy was sleeping.
   While he was outside, John saw a fire truck.

(e) **NP$_s$ - Pro**
   Because Jenna saw a mouse, she ran away.
   While Tom was riding the horse, he looked around.

(continued)

Notice that not all the (at least logically) possible intercombinations of main/ subordinate clause and coreferential NP/Pron are represented in this schema. There is actually a very good reason for this deriving from a principle encountered in Part I, Section C.

1. Very simply, which of the four logically possible intercombinations was not used in Lust's experiment and what would be an example of a sentence representing such a combination?

2. What problem of interpretation is evident in such an example?

3. Can you think of a principle that might be at work here and how it relates to the facts of interpretation?

ASSIGNMENT 94** **Binding Theory**

Consider once more the nature of the grammatical categories termed **anaphor** and **pronoun,** introduced in Assignment 92. Coindexing of an anaphor and a pronoun with an antecedent in each of the following examples leads to grammaticality with one and ungrammaticality with the other. A relevant observation follows each example or set of examples:

   $Mary_i$ likes $herself_i/*her_i$
   $Sally_i$ believes [that $Mary$ likes $*herself_i/her_i$]
   $Sally$ believes [$Mary_i$ to like $herself_i/*her_i$]

- **Domain of anaphor + antecedent is ± finite clause**

   $Mary_i$'s brother likes $*herself_i/her_i$
- **Anaphor must have a c-commanding antecedent**

   $Mary_i$, Max likes $*herself_i/her_i$
- **Antecedent of anaphor must be in an A(rgument)-Position**

   $Mary_i$ believes [that $*herself_i/she_i$ is liked]
- **Anaphor/subject of finite clause requires local c-commanding antecedent**

   $Mary_i$ believes [$herself_i/*her_i$ (to be) liked]
- **C-commanding antecedent for anaphor/subject of non-finite/small clause can be non-local**

   $Mary_i$ believes [that the picture of $herself_i/?her_i$ is liked]
- **Antecedent for anaphor-within-subject can be non-local**

Examples like these have led to the statement of principles of **binding,** represented above in the coindexing:

- **Principle A:** An anaphor is bound in its local domain.

- **Principle B:** A pronoun is free in its local domain.

- **Principle C:** An R(eferential)-expression is free everywhere.

(continued)

Each of the examples below, considered as ungrammatical, runs afoul of one of the principles of binding theory. State briefly what principle (A, B, C) has been violated and in what way.

1. *John believes that Mary$_i$ hurt her$_i$
   Principle . . .:

   . . . .

2. *Herself$_i$ hurt Mary$_i$
   Principle . . .:

   . . . .

3. *John's$_i$ mother hurt himself$_i$
   Principle . . .:

   . . . .

4. *Will somebody$_i$ please talk to him$_i$
   Principle . . .:

   . . . .

5. *John$_i$ doesn't like Mary's picture of himself$_i$
   Principle . . .:

   . . . .

6. *He$_i$ knows that John$_i$ won't come
   Principle . . .:

   . . . .

7. *Mary$_i$ hurt himself$_i$
   Principle . . .:

   . . . .

8. *John$_i$ guessed that Mary hurt himself$_i$
   Principle . . .:

   . . . .

9. *John$_i$, she didn't hurt himself$_i$
   Principle . . .:

   . . . .

10. *We didn't expect himself$_i$ to hurt John$_i$
    Principle . . .:

    . . . .

ASSIGNMENT **Binding Theory: L1**
95*

One of the classic studies of child language acquisition is that of C. Chomsky (1969), a useful discussion of which can be found in Ingram (1989: 488–90). Briefly, Chomsky conducted an experiment to determine how 40 children aged 5 to 10 process three types of construction, represented here using both Ingram's labels and the English examples cited (coreference indices added here):

Type 1:   **Blocked backward pronominalization**
*He_i found out that Mickey_i won the race

Type 2:   **Backward pronominalization**
Before he_i went out, Pluto_i took a nap

Type 3:   **Forward pronominalization**
Pluto_i thinks he_i knows everything

By Principle B of the Binding Theory, all three examples are of course possible sentences if non-coreferentiality obtains. Furthermore, all but type 1 allow a coreferential interpretation, disallowed for type 1 because of a Principle C violation (namely, the noun *Mickey* is c-commanded by its coreferential pronoun *he*). Although the results of Chomsky's experiment showed that 78 percent of the children correctly ruled out the coreferential interpretation for type 1, four of these same children also failed to provide coreferential responses for type 2. Very simply, what strategy could these four children have been employing in their responses?

ASSIGNMENT 96*** Binding Theory: GCP

Antecedents for reflexives are found cross-linguistically within a defined range of syntactic structures. For a given language the structure in question is often referred to as the **governing category** for the reflexive in that language. (The less precise term used in Assignment 94 was **local domain**.) Cross-linguistic variation in choice of governing category indicates that it is parameterized, the term adopted being the **Governing Category Parameter**, or **GCP**. The GCP is defined as follows (with a sample language associated with each value of the parameter):

α is a governing category for β if and only if α is the minimal category which contains β and

(a)	has a subject, or	[English]
(b)	has an INFL, or	[Italian]
(c)	has a TNS, or	[Russian]
(d)	has an indicative TNS, or	[Icelandic]
(e)	has a root TNS	[Japanese, Korean]

Another way of displaying the five values, this time using English, would be the following, where the actual letters of the five settings (a)–(e) are used as subscripts for coindexing with the reflexive, indexed as "x":

Keith$_e$ **said**
  root TNS

  [that Ronnie$_d$ **requires**
        indic TNS

     [that Bill$_c$ **persuade** Charlie
           TNS

        [PRO$_b$ **to consider**
              INFL

           [**Mick**$_a$ fond of Self$_x$]]]]
           subject

(continued)

Since the five values of the GCP define a relationship of **inclusion** (i.e. each category, going from top to bottom, is a subset of the next), they also represent a scale of **markedness**, with value (a) being least marked and value (e) most marked. Note that the English reflexive has value (a) of the parameter; the anaphoric elements of other languages range themselves at different points in the hierarchy, as in the above sample.

Imagine for a moment that English adopts instead the MOST marked value (e) of the GCP. For the five sentences below (taken from Finer 1991), indicate how each in turn might represent one of the five parametric values by writing one of the values (a)–(e) next to the sentence and coindexing the reflexive with the antecedent in question. Since the five values define relationships of inclusion, choose each example in terms of the WIDEST possible coindexing.

1. ... *Starsky considers Hutch fond of Self*$_i$

2. ... *Ward requires that Wally be polite to Self*$_i$

3. ... *Curly stole Moe's pictures of Self*$_i$

4. ... *Alex doesn't care that Krystle dislikes Self*$_i$

5. ... *Fred expected Barney to invite Self*$_i$ *to lunch*

ASSIGNMENT 97* **Binding Theory: GCP and L2**

Look once again at the facts concerning the **Governing Category Parameter** as displayed in the previous assignment. Several studies have so far been conducted that are designed to examine a learner's knowledge of the GCP setting appropriate to another language being learned in adulthood. Lee (1992) undertook an extensive study of the acquisition of L2 English reflexive binding by Korean L1 learners of various ages and lengths of exposure to English. Her older subjects tended to judge sentences like *John remembered that I had helped himself* and *Mary expected John to give flowers to herself* as grammatical and to choose both nouns as possible antecedents for the reflexive in sentences like *Tom discovered that John had hit himself* and *Alice remembered Mary's speech about herself.*

Given that English is associated with value (a) of the GCP and Korean with value (e), and with nothing else at the moment to go on, what preliminary guesses would you want to make concerning the acquisition of L2 English reflexive binding by adult native speakers of Korean? What potential L2 learning problem do these data point to?

ASSIGNMENT 98** Binding Theory and DP/NP: L1

The binding principles A, B, and C introduced in Assignment 94 are repeated here for convenience:

- **Principle A**: An anaphor is bound in its local domain.

- **Principle B**: A pronoun is free in its local domain.

- **Principle C**: An R(eferential)-expression is free everywhere.

With reference to principles A and B in particular, consider the following examples:

(a)   *Max$_i$ took a picture of himself$_i$*

(b)   **Max$_i$ took a picture of him$_i$*

(c)   *Max$_i$ took the picture of him$_i$*

The coreferential interpretation for *Max* and the anaphor *himself* in (a) is licensed by Principle A. Conversely, the coreferential interpretation for *Max* and the pronoun *him* in (b) is disallowed by Principle B. What then of (c)? Recall from Assignment 8 the claim that **indefinites** like *a picture* can be interpreted as either **specific** or **non-specific**, according to context, and that specific indefinites are to be analyzed as **DPs**, non-specific indefinites as **NPs**. DPs introduce a new local domain for binding purposes; NPs do not. *A picture* ... in both (a) and (b) is non-specific and therefore an NP, which permits coreference with the anaphor in (a) but not the pronoun in (b). However, *the picture* ... in (c) is a DP, introducing a new local domain for the pronoun, and therefore coreference is licensed by Principle B.

With these DP/NP observations in mind and recalling the barriers to wh-extraction and the subjacency phenomenon discussed in Assignment 42, consider the following:

(d)   *Who$_i$ did Max take a picture of t$_i$?*

(e)   ?*Who$_i$ did Max take a picture of t$_i$?*

(continued)

Name: _____   Date: __ / __ / __   Class: _____

In that same assignment were sets of examples suggesting contrasts identified as "unusual" – contrasts such as:

(f) *What did you **claim** that he said* t_i?

(g) ?*What*$_i$ *did you **make the claim** that he said* t_i?

(h) *What$_i$ *did you **file the claim** that he said* t_i?

The verb in expressions like *make the claim, have the feeling, reach a decision*, etc., has been termed **light verb**, in that it is the complement rather than the verb that seems to carry the semantic weight: *make the claim = claim; have the feeling = feel; reach a decision = decide*, etc. Bear in mind, however, that the "unusualness" of light-verb behavior ranges beyond subjacency phenomena. The passivization in (i), for example, provides a contrast analogous to that of (g) and (h):

(i) *The decision was **reached/*liked** to go ahead*

We noted above that the binding constraints evident in (a)–(c) seem to be rooted in the DP/NP distinction. It has been suggested that the subjacency/ barrier constraints evident in (d)–(h) also reduce to the DP/NP distinction (cf. de Villiers and Roeper 1995). Briefly, how would the DP/NP contrast relate to the judgements in contrasting grammaticality displayed in (d)–(e) and (f)–(h)? (Note that with complements to light verbs, the choice of definite or indefinite article is irrelevant for analytical purposes.)

It has been seen in a number of these assignments (e.g. Assignment 9) that children are conservative learners, in that they expand their grammatical systems only upon reaching the awareness of positive evidence for doing so. If children thus start out conservatively, what kinds of interpretation would you therefore predict they will show with regard to the binding and barrier constraints exemplified in the above sentences?

Binding Theory and Relativization

Consider the following sentence containing a relative clause in which there is coreference between a pronoun in the main clause and its antecedent in the relative clause:

*Which pictures that **John**$_i$ took does **he**$_i$ like?*

Consider now the underlying representation of this sentence BEFORE wh-movement to form the question:

he$_i$ *(does) like [which pictures that **John**$_i$ took]*

whose tree would look something like this:

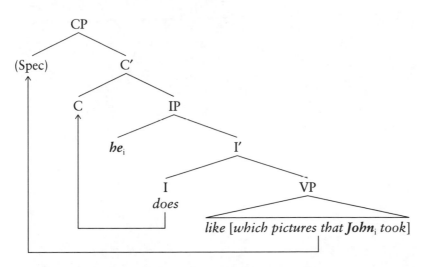

It has been suggested by Lebeaux (1990) that this analysis of relative clause structure poses a problem with respect to binding theory. Lebeaux proposes that the underlying structure of this sentence is actually the following:

he (does) like [which pictures]

(continued)

where initially the relative clause *that John took* does not appear at all and is instead **inserted** into the structure AFTER wh-movement. (See Assignment 57.)

Briefly then, what is the problem for the conventional analysis of relative clauses posed by the above sentence and how is the problem solved by adopting Lebeaux's analysis?

PART IV

Typology

SECTION A Word Order

ASSIGNMENT 100* Canonical Word Order: English

Mark each of the following English sentences (main clause only) in terms of its SURFACE canonical word order (e.g. V, S, O). Some sentences do not of course contain all three major constituents. Represent as "X" any arguments that are not "O".

For example:

	Into the valley rode the six hundred.	*XVS* . . . .
1.	*Really good meals they serve at that hotel.*	. . . .
2.	*They gave everybody a really warm welcome.*	. . . .
3.	*This latter topic we have examined in chapter 3.*	. . . .
4.	*To this list may be added ten additional items.*	. . . .
5.	*His face not many admired.*	. . . .
6.	*One tree does not a forest make.*	. . . .
7.	*Into the stifling smoke we plunged.*	. . . .
8.	*Into the stifling smoke plunged the fire brigade.*	. . . .
9.	*Here comes my brother.*	. . . .
10.	*"Please go away," said one child.*	. . . .
11.	*Said the governor, "You see one redwood . . ."*	. . . .
12.	*Who did it?*	. . . .
13.	*That he would do a thing like that disturbs me.*	. . . .
14.	*It disturbs me for them to think that about us.*	. . . .
15.	*"Irks care the crop-full bird?*	. . . .
	Frets doubt the maw-crammed beast?" (Browning)	. . . .
16.	*"Great oaks from little acorns grow."* (old saying)	. . . .
17.	*In the garden stood a sundial.*	. . . .
18.	*Such delightful children they raised!*	. . . .
19.	*We despise them, those politicians.*	. . . .
20.	*Put your coat in the closet.*	. . . .

Word Order: General

(data from Greenberg 1963)

Linguists working within the generative model distinguish between **heads** of phrases and their **satellites** – i.e. complements and adjuncts (Assignment 22). This fundamental distinction has long been recognized, however, by linguists working within other theories of grammar and a classic example is to be found in the contribution of Joseph Greenberg. Language typologists such as Greenberg were able to ascertain degrees of consistency among vast numbers of languages by examining the positions of phrasal heads in those languages relative to their complements and adjuncts. The terms preferred by typologists in this instance are **operand** (for head) and **operator** (for satellite). Accordingly, the relationship, for example, of a relative clause to its head noun is one of operator to operand; thus, in English the order is operand–operator, whereas in say Japanese it is the reverse.

With reference then to the order of operator vis-à-vis operand, decide which of the languages cited below show(s) the most consistency and which show(s) the least consistency. The abbreviations stand for S[ubject], O[bject], V[erb], Po[stposition], Pr[eposition], Rel[ative clause], N[oun], G[enitive], A[djective].

Basque	SOV	/	Po	/	Rel N	/	GN	/	NA
Guarani	SVO	/	Po	/	N Rel	/	GN	/	NA
Turkish	SOV	/	Po	/	Rel N	/	GN	/	AN
English	SVO	/	Pr	/	N Rel	/	GN	/	AN
Spanish	SVO	/	Pr	/	N Rel	/	NG	/	NA
Zapotec	VSO	/	Pr	/	N Rel	/	NG	/	NA
Maya	SVO	/	Pr	/	N Rel	/	NG	/	AN
Persian	SOV	/	Pr	/	N Rel	/	NG	/	NA

most consistent: ....

least consistent: ....

ASSIGNMENT 102** Word Order and Code-Switching

There are many languages that we could have used as examples of word order (i.e. operand/operator or head/satellite) consistency, or inconsistency, in addition to those displayed in the previous assignment. Japanese, for example, is SOV, Po, Rel N, GN, and AN – that is, fully consistent in terms of left-branching typology. With respect to a significant group of major structures, Japanese and English therefore show a "mirror image" relation, as noted by Nishimura (1986):

English	Japanese
VO	OV
there V NP	NP V [existential]
P NP	NP P
Comp S	S particle

The Nishimura paper provides the following examples of Japanese/English **code-switching** in which a Japanese sentence and an English sentence are combined via a shared element (*italicized*) – an **operator** in typological terms – not unlike the reported tendency of monolingual English speakers to occasionally say things like "That's *the only thing he does* is fight":

(a)   We bought about *two pounds* GURAI KATTEKITA NO
                                                    about   bought

(b)   Let's become *KECHI* NI NAROO
                           tight   become

(c)   There's *children* IRU YO
                                V [existential]

(d)   Look at the things she buys for *Sean* NI
                                                               for

(continued)

Name: _____ Date: __ / __ / __ Class: _____

Notice that the examples are ones in which the sentence starts in English and finishes in Japanese. In fact, ALL the instances of such combining in Nishimura's database exhibited this ordering. Why should this be? What aspect of contrasting word-order typology for Japanese and English might plausibly render it unlikely that code-switching sentences of this kind (i.e. with a shared **operator**) would ever begin in Japanese and end in English?

ASSIGNMENT
103*

Word Order and Clitics: L2

English speakers learning French often pass through a stage of development where they produce sentences like *Je vois le*, before finally learning the correct *Je le vois* ("I see him"). French learners of English, however, do *not* pass through an analogous stage of development where they produce sentences like *I him see* on the way to the correct *I see him*. Similarly, English speakers learning Spanish often produce sentences like *La policía quiere él* before the correct *La policía lo quiere* ("The police want him"), whereas Spanish learners of English have not been observed to produce a developmental *The police him want*. If the starred French and Spanish examples are to be attributed to transfer from English, then why does transfer not work the other way as well to produce the (non-occurring) starred English examples? Look for an explanation in terms of canonical word order and branching direction.

Name: _____   Date: __ / __ / __   Class: _____

<hr>

ASSIGNMENT   # Word-Order
104*   # Typology (I)

One of the ways in which typologists attempt to classify human languages is in terms of the order in which their **canonical** or most "basic" constituents occur, the constituents in question being S[ubject], O[bject], and V[erb]. The number of possible permutations of these three constituents comes to six: **SOV, SVO, VSO, OSV, OVS, VOS,** where the first three of these account for more than 95 percent of the world's languages.

Generativists recognize these orders but generate them largely through the interaction of two parameters, the **Comp(lement)–head parameter** and the **Spec(ifier)–head parameter,** each having the option of the head either preceding or following its satellite (namely, Comp or Spec). Thus, the Comp–head parameter can be set to yield either an OV or VO order and the Spec–head parameter settings can result in the S either preceding the VP (i.e. V + O) or following it.

Taking this four-way parametric intercombination into account, plot as many of the six canonical orders as these options permit, using the framework below. Under the two parameters, enter either "head-initial" or "head-final" for each of the generable canonical orders.

SPECIFIER/HEAD	COMPLEMENT/HEAD	WORD ORDER
. . . .	. . . .	SOV
. . . .	. . . .	SVO
. . . .	. . . .	VSO
. . . .	. . . .	OSV
. . . .	. . . .	OVS
. . . .	. . . .	VOS

Name: _____   Date: __ / __ / __   Class: _____

ASSIGNMENT **Word-Order**
105** Typology (II)

Refer once more to the Spec–head and Comp–head parameter settings for the
six word orders listed in the previous assignment. You will have deduced, for
example, that SOV is the result of a head-final setting for the Spec–head parameter and a head-final setting for the Comp–head parameter. Consider now
what orders will result if we add to this language the positive setting of another
parameter – namely, **verb-second** or **V2**: the addition of [+V2] will now yield
SVO and SV. Suppose further that we add in the auxiliary or **AUX** (whose
position can satisfy the V2 requirement): we now have, in addition to SVO and
SV, S AUX V, S AUX O V, and O AUX S V. Now add in still another factor
– namely, the licensing of sentence-initial adverbs (**ADV**). In addition to all the
orders just cited, we now obtain ADV V S, ADV AUX S V, ADV AUX S O V,
and so on. These parameter settings (plus initial ADV) are in fact those of, for
example, German.

Cited below are the parameter settings for two different languages, with a
composite set of word-order possibilities for the two listed on the right. For each
of the two languages, check the word orders that are actually defined by its
parameter settings.

(continued)

269

Name: _____   Date: __ / __ / __   Class: _____

	LANGUAGE 1	LANGUAGE 2	
Spec–head parameter:	Head-initial	Head-final	
Comp–head parameter:	Head-initial	Head-initial	
Verb-second parameter:	[+V2]	[–V2]	
	S-initial ADV	S-initial ADV	
	✓.	✓.	1. S V O
	. . .	. . .	2. S V
	. ⁄.	. . .	3. O V S
	. . .	. . .	4. S AUX V O
	. . .	. . .	5. S AUX V
	. . .	. . .	6. O AUX V S
	. . .	. . .	7. ADV V O S
	. . .	. . .	8. ADV V S
	. . .	. . .	9. ADV AUX V O S
	. . .	. . .	10. ADV AUX V S
	. . .	. . .	11. ADV S V O
	. . .	. . .	12. ADV S V
	. . .	. . .	13. ADV S AUX V O
	. . .	. . .	14. ADV S AUX V

ASSIGNMENT
106***

Word-Order Typology: L2

Refer once more to the previous assignment. Assume a learning situation for some adult language learner in which Language 1 is her native language and Language 2 is the new language being learned. This would be a language contact situation in which the two languages contrast on two of the three parameter settings at issue here. Suppose the learner imagines, before starting out, that the L2 **representational system** is the same as that of her native language. And suppose she then initially encounters in the L2 input only strings of the form SVO, SV, S AUX V O, and S AUX V. At this point, what assumptions about the target language is the learner likely to hold? What possible learnability problem would thereby ensue?

(continued)

271

Suppose now that the learner encounters in the L2 input the order ADV S V O, one which is ungrammatical in her native language, and attempts to adjust the grammar of the target language by changing the value of one of the three parameter settings (and where only one value may be changed at a time). What serious learnability problem has the learner now encountered and what might be a possible solution?

SECTION B Subject- and Topic-Prominence

Topic/Subject Characteristics

One of the typologies that have been proposed for cross-linguistic classification of languages is that of **Topic-Prominence (T-P)** vs. **Subject-Prominence (S-P)**. In T-P languages the category **topic**, in contrast to **subject**, figures crucially in basic sentence structure. Chinese is a good example of this. In S-P languages basic sentence structure is built instead around the category **subject**, although **topicalization** devices may also be utilized (cf. Assignment 34). English is a good example of this. Japanese and Korean show characteristics of both. Consider the topic and/ or subject in the two groups of examples below – one Chinese (a) and one Japanese (b), both with English glosses – and make mental notes concerning such concepts as definiteness, coding, agreement, coreference, selectional restrictions, etc.

(a) (i)   **Neike shu, hua   xiao, yezi   da, hen nankan, (suoyi)**
           That tree flower small leaves big very ugly   so
           wo mei mai
           I   not buy

           "The tree, (its) flowers are small; (its) leaves are big; (it) is very ugly: (so that) I did not buy (it)"

     (ii) *****Zheixie xuesheng, Lisi jiaoguo, meiyou jiaoguo neixie**
           These   student   Lisi teach   not   teach those

           "These students, Lisi has taught, (but he) has not taught those"

     (iii) **Zheixie xuesheng, Lisi jiaoguo, wo ye   jiaoguo**
           These   student   Lisi teach   I   also teach

           "These students, Lisi has taught, (and) I have taught, too"

(b) (i)   **John wa   gakusei desu**
           John TOPIC student is

           "Speaking of John, he is a student"

     (ii) **John ga   gakusei desu**
           John SUBJECT student is

           "John is a student" (neutral description)

(continued)

(iii) **Kono hon wa John ga yonda**
This book TOPIC John SUBJECT read

"Speaking of this book, John has read it"

(iv) **Ginkoo ni itta hito wa dare desu ka?**
Bank to went person TOPIC who is QUESTION

"Who is the person who went to the bank?"

With reference to whatever observations you have been able to make concerning the above data, and in consideration of what you already know about English, try to determine whether the following features characterize subjects or topics, or possibly both:

	SUBJECT	TOPIC
1. obligatorily definite	...	✓.
2. obligatory selectional restrictions with verb	...	...
3. grammatical function constant across sentences	...	...
4. obligatory agreement with verb	...	...
5. sentence-initial position	...	...
6. prominent role in syntactic processes	...	...
7. surface marking possible	...	...
8. "dummy" elements as grammatical place-holders	...	...
9. control of coreferential constituent deletion	...	...
10. no semantic constraints on what it may be	...	...
11. perceived as a discourse notion	...	...
12. case-marked	...	...
13. identified as argument of verb	...	...

ASSIGNMENT 108** Topicalization: L1

In one of the classic studies of child language acquisition, Gruber (1967) makes a strong claim that the child's earliest utterances should be analyzed as **topic–comment** rather than **subject–predicate**. There then would be a gradual shift to subject–predicate in the child's further development toward target (final state) English, whereas topic–comment would continue to prevail for, say, target Chinese. The data that figure in the analysis are all from English and will be grouped in the following manner:

(A) Roughly equal distribution of X NP and NP X:

(1a)	go way wheels	(1b)	girl go away
(2a)	over there train	(2b)	choo choo over there
(3a)	all broken wheel	(3b)	dump truck all fixed
(4a)	break pumpkin	(4b)	other wheel broke
(5a)	in there wheels	(5b)	pony in there
(6a)	there's the truck	(6b)	motor in the car
(7a)	there's the wheel	(7b)	fire truck there
(8a)	go truck	(8b)	Mama goes
(9a)	go in there train	(9b)	wheels move
(10a)	it broken, wheels	(10b)	car, it broken

(B) Examples of case-marked and non-case-marked pronouns:

(1a)	I wanna	(1b)	me wanna truck
(2a)	he take the wheels, fire engine	(2b)	me take the wheel
(3a)	I show you?	(3b)	me show you?
(4a)	I write	(4b)	me draw
(5a)	see the tree	(5b)	him go right back
(6a)	bites anyone	(6b)	no him no bite
		(7b)	catch me (= "I can catch it")

He's a bad him

(continued)

(C) Pronoun case-marking and the copula:

Occurring		Possible		Not occurring	
(1a)	*him bear*	(1b)	*he dog*		
(2a)	*him bad dog*	(2b)	*he's dog*	(2c)	**him's a bad dog*
(3a)	*them eyes*	(3b)	*he's a dog*	(3c)	**him is a bad dog*
(4a)	*me no bear*	(4b)	*he is a dog*	(4c)	**is a dog*

(5a) *I'm go*
(6a) *He's put*

(D) Appearing in isolation:

   (i)   nouns
   (ii) *him, them, me* / **he, *she, *they, *it, *I*

(E) In addition, note the following:

   (i)   The recorded adult language to which the child was exposed con-
         tained no examples of **topicalization** or **left dislocation**.
   (ii) There were no examples of a verb followed by a non-case-marked
         pronoun subject (*he/she/I*).
   (iii) The child's *I/he/it* occur only in subject position; *he's* is analyzed as
         another form of *he*, *I'm* another form of *I*.

State briefly how the data and the observations taken together can support the
claim that many of the child's utterances are to be analyzed as **topic–comment**.
Which of the above data would have to be analyzed as **subject–predicate**?

ASSIGNMENT 109* Topics and Pseudo-Passives (Informal): L2

The sentences below are all examples of an English interlanguage construction typically produced by Mandarin speakers (Yip 1995). This kind of construction is often diagnosed, before careful analysis, as a failed attempt by the learner to produce an English **passive**, often referred to as a **pseudo-passive**. The intended target form for item 1, for example, would therefore supposedly be *Most of the food which is served in such a restaurant **has been cooked** already*. Yet, it cannot be that the learner in this case does not know the English passive, because a CORRECT instance of the passive is to be seen in this very same example: ... *which is served* ... Rather, it is far more plausible, given that Mandarin is a **topic-prominent** language, to consider the IL example as manifesting a **topic-comment** structure, something perhaps like the following:

> **Topic:** *Most of food ... restaurant*
> **Comment:** *(I/we/they/one) have cooked [it] already*

Examine the rest of the sentences in similar fashion and represent their structures informally as in no. 1.

1. *Most of food which is served in such restaurant have cooked already*

   Most of food ... restaurant (we/etc.) have cooked [it] already.

2. *Irrational emotions are bad but rational emotions must use for judging*

   . . . .

3. *Chiang's food must make in the kitchen of the restaurant but Marty's food could make in his house*

   . . . .

4. *If I have finished these four jobs, I am confident that my company can list in the biggest 100 companies in the world*

   . . . .

5. *These ways almost can classify two types*

   . . . .

(continued)

6. *We do know that as soon as the transportation network has finished, we can advance*

    . . . .

7. *New cars must keep indoors*

    . . . .

Name: _____   Date: _ / _ / _   Class: _____

ASSIGNMENT 110* Topics and Pseudo-Passives (Formal): L2

Consider once more the IL construction exemplified in the previous assignment, wherein a **topic–comment** analysis is preferred to a **pseudo-passive** one. Assuming for now that **topic** is derived rather than base-generated, represent the original IL examples in formal terms along something like the lines suggested for item one, where **TOP** is the utterance-initial constituent and **pro** stands in for a missing subject (cf. Assignment 115).

1. *Most of food which is served in such restaurant have cooked already*
   [$_{TOP}$ *most of food . . . restaurant$_i$*] [$_{IP}$ *[pro] have cooked* [t_i] *already*]

2. *Irrational emotions are bad but rational emotions must use for judging*

   . . . .

3. *Chiang's food must make in the kitchen of the restaurant but Marty's food could make in his house*

   . . . .

4. *If I have finished these four jobs, I am confident that my company can list in the biggest 100 companies in the world*

   . . . .

5. *These ways almost can classify two types*

   . . . .

6. *We do know that as soon as the transportation network has finished, we can advance*

   . . . .

7. *New cars must keep indoors*

   . . . .

Name: _____   Date: __ / __ / __   Class: _____

ASSIGNMENT 111* From Topic to Subject: L2

The three sentences below are taken from written production by adult intermediate-level Mandarin speakers studying English at an American university. The changes that appear are actually those made by the learners and are exactly as they appeared in the original writing samples. In what way can these emendations be taken as evidence that the learners' IL **representational system** is in the process of **typological** reanalysis – i.e. presumably from **topic–prominence** to **subject–prominence**? It will be of help to recall that initial NPs in (topic-prominent) Mandarin must be **definite**.

1. There are *A* lot of male and female students. Make friend in school

2. Some people personality *'s* *is* not easy to find a husband or wife

3. In a coeducational school, there are many students have *ing* this good opportunity

ASSIGNMENT 112*   Topic and Determiner: L2 (data from Jain 1974)

The following passage of English interlanguage is cited without identification of the learner's mother tongue. Consider the positions where the **definite article** is obligatory and note whether the learner has used or not used it. What observations can you now make concerning presence/absence of the definite article as deployed by this particular learner? Would you want to hazard a guess as to the **typological** identity of the learner's L1? (The numbers identify the clausal material.)

In the meantime ¹the driver stopped the engine. ²He tried to start it again when ³the conductor whistled. ⁴Engine did not start. In the meantime, ⁵conductor decided to check the bus. ⁶Conductor asked me about my ticket; ⁷I had not bought it by then. ⁸I asked the conductor for the ticket. By now ⁹engine was on; then ¹⁰he whistled and ¹¹bus went away.

ASSIGNMENT 113** Topic-Prominence and the Determiner: L2

One of the classic L2 longitudinal studies is that of Huebner (1979), who looked at (among other things) acquisition of the English determiner system by a native speaker of Hmong, a **topic-prominent** language of Southeast Asia. Huebner's system for coding the determiner utilized two binary features: [+/−specific referent] and [+/−assumed hearer's knowledge]. This four-way distinction thus yielded the following possibilities for NPs:

(1)   +Spec +H = **unique, previous mention**   [... *a child* ...] *the child*

(2)   −Spec +H = **generic**   *Children are fun*

(3)   −Spec −H = **non-specific indefinite**   [... *a/any child* ...] *one*

(4)   +Spec −H = **specific indefinite**   [... *a (certain) child* ...] *him*

The following table shows the distribution of *da* (= *the*), *a*, and Ø in four environments of the learner's IL over a one-year period, divided into four time intervals (T):

	[+Specific +Hearer]			[−Specific +Hearer]			[−Specific −Hearer]			[+Specific −Hearer]		
T4	154	2	22	1	0	10	3	9	40	13	8	23
T3	199	2	13	0	0	7	3	12	27	32	8	8
T2	133	0	40	1	0	4	3	5	56	33	0	2
T1	67	1	47	2	0	4	4	2	35	2	12	18
	(1.) *da*	*a*	Ø	(2.) *da*	*a*	Ø	(3.) *da*	*a*	Ø	(4.) *da*	*a*	Ø

Although the above table cites tabulations for all four NP types, what we will be concerned with here is that for type 1: [+**Specific, +Hearer**]. There are several things worth noting regarding this particular data set. The percentage of type 1 NP at T1 marked with *da* is low; yet the distribution is not random: of the 67 instances of [+Spec/+H], ONLY 7 ARE SUBJECT. Of the other 48 (47 + 1) for type 1, 30 ARE SUBJECT. Thus, the learner marks a [+Spec/+H] NP with *da* except in **subject** position. It needs to be mentioned also that production of *a* at T1 in environment 4 is epenthetic (i.e. *have* .... NP). Thus there are virtually no indefinite articles at T1.

(continued)

On the basis of these observations, what conclusion would you draw concerning the typological status of the learner's IL at T1 and why?

SECTION C Null-Subject

ASSIGNMENT 114* Missing Subjects

It was noted in Assignment 63 that English allows sentences to be shortened along the following lines:

> *Have you seen any good movies lately?*
> *'vyou seen any good movies lately?*
> *You seen any good movies lately?*
> *Seen any good movies lately?*

But not:

(a) **Have   seen any good movies lately?*

Data like these indicate that it is generally impossible in English for the pronoun subject NOT to appear. Compare this ungrammatical English example (a) with its counterparts in Italian (b) and Spanish (c):

(b) *Ha   visto qualche bel   film   di recente?*
(c) *Ha   visto alguna   buena pelicula recentemente?*
     have(3sg) seen any   good movies   lately

For these three languages, note further the verb paradigms – in this case for auxiliary *have*:

	English	Italian	Spanish
1st sg	*have*	*ho*	*he*
2nd	*have*	*hai*	*has*
3rd	*has*	*ha*	*ha*
1st pl	*have*	*abbiamo*	*hemos*
2nd	*have*	*avete*	*habéis*
3rd	*have*	*hanno*	*han*

Intuitively, what feature do languages like Italian and Spanish have such that sentences in these languages with missing pronoun subjects are perfectly interpretable?

ASSIGNMENT 115*** Null-Subject: L1

It was demonstrated in the previous assignment that languages like Italian and Spanish with full verbal inflection have the option, unlike English, of omitting unstressed pronominal subjects. The inflection in question is the bundle of agreement features (Agr) encoded in I (NFL), which are rich enough to permit an interpretable null element – namely **pro** – to stand in for overt pronoun subjects. The Italian and English representations for *Have you seen any good movies lately?* would thus be (a) and (b):

(a) $[_{CP} [_C$ *Have* $[_{IP}$ **you** .... *seen any good movies lately*$]]]$

(b) $[_{CP} [_C$ *Ha*$_i$ $[_{IP}$ **pro**$_i$ .... *visto qualche bel film di recente*$]]]$

Languages, like Italian and Spanish, which license the omission of unstressed (subject) pronouns are called **null-subject** or **pro-drop**, this feature being identified as a parameter of Universal Grammar whose settings are [± **pro-drop**]. Although English is [– pro-drop], the null-subject feature is often seen in colloquial spoken English with sentences like *Saw a good movie yesterday*, where the dropped element is interpretable from context as "I" or "we" and has been analyzed as more **topic** than subject. Declarative sentence versions analogous to (a) and (b) could therefore be (a′) and (b′):

(a′) **[Pro]** *saw a good movie yesterday* (= "I/we saw . . .")

(b′) **[Pro**$_i$**]** *ho*$_i$ *visto ieri un bel film*
                have(1sg)

It has generally been observed by L1 acquisition researchers that children's utterances at an early stage and in whatever language appear to manifest the null-subject characteristic, as shown in the following examples for English produced by one child at age 20–2 months:

watch noise	*want more apple*
need shoes	*eat juice*
build house	*shake hands*
make pee	*show me*
get it	*eating cereal*

(continued)

Researchers differ, however, as to what accounting to give data of this kind. Two well-defined positions have emerged:

(A) **Children's early grammars are DIFFERENT from those of adults in that they are all initially [+ pro-drop] and subsequently switch to [– pro-drop] for those adult languages that have that setting.**

(B) **Children's early grammars are the SAME as those of adults vis-à-vis [± pro-drop]; the apparent discrepancy, where missing subjects are concerned, is attributable to performance factors – i.e. either informativeness (subjects tending to be presupposed, less informative, etc.) or processing.**

Listed below are a number of the observations about child language that have been cited in support of one or the other of these two positions. Indicate which of the positions you think the observation supports by writing (A) or (B) in the space provided. Assume, for the purposes of this assignment, that an argument AGAINST one position can be taken as support FOR the other. Note also that an observation might in some cases be construed as support for BOTH positions. Can you offer a REASON for your choice?

1. (   ) Most of children's early utterances are less than three words long.

2. (   ) A young child uses a null subject where an older child or adult will use a pronoun.

3. (   ) Children omit all kinds of constituents, not just subjects.

4. (   ) Children's early grammars show far more null subjects than null objects.

5. (   ) In the acquisition of a [– pro-drop] language, there may be a relationship between the disappearance of null subjects and the manifestation of a range of other properties claimed to be formally associated with the pro-drop parameter.

(continued)

6. (   ) Children are claimed to drop subjects more with transitive verbs than intransitive verbs.

7. (   ) Children who drop subjects produce longer utterances.

8. (   ) Very young English acquirers omit pronoun subjects much less frequently than young Italian acquirers.

9. (   ) Even when children try to IMITATE perfectly understandable adult speech, the length of the imitation is limited.

10. (   ) Some children simply REDUCE the subject to a schwa [ə].

Name: _____   Date: __ / __ / __   Class: _____

ASSIGNMENT 116**

Word Order and Null-Subject: L2

(data from Rutherford 1987a)

In analyzing great quantities of languages over the years, researchers have needed to devise a number of different typologies to account for ways in which languages are similar and ways in which they differ. One of the widely utilized typologies is that of basic ordering of the canonical sentence constituents S, O, and V (cf. Section A). Another would be the basic structure of sentences as either topic–comment or subject–predicate, or indeed both (cf. Section B). Still another would be the propensity of languages to allow, or disallow, the suppression of pronoun subjects (the present section). The last typology we will mention here, one closely related to the licensing of null-subjects, is the tendency for languages to order their basic sentence constituents in accord with either grammatical criteria or pragmatic criteria. Languages obeying the former are said to be typologically **Grammatical Word Order (GWO)**, the latter **Pragmatic Word Order (PWO)**, GWO and PWO actually marking the two ends of a continuum along which the world's languages theoretically may range. English is a very good example of GWO, Spanish of PWO.

Pairs of sentences, one from each language, will offer a glimpse at the contrast – where, as context, someone named "Mary/Maria" is wrongly presupposed to have sent a certain letter:

(a)	*Sent the letter John	Envió la carta Juan
(b)	JOHN sent the letter	?JUAN envió la carta
(c)	The letter was sent by John	?La carta fue enviado por Juan
(d)	It was John who sent the letter	?Fue Juan que envió la carta

John/Juan is the **rhematically** salient element in these sentences (cf. Assignment 130) and the saliency in spoken English would typically be accomplished through (rigid) SVO order with stress on S (*John*). In spoken Spanish, however, it would typically be accomplished simply through (flexible) reordering of SVO to VOS, thus placing *Juan* in sentence-final, salient position. It is important to recognize that the goal in both instances has been the same: according discourse prominence to a canonical sentence constituent, in this case the subject. Spanish can

(continued)

achieve it simply by rearranging the constituents such that the subject is placed last. English can also achieve it by putting the subject last, as in (c), but, crucially, must utilize a grammatical device – namely, passive – to do so, wherein grammatical-subject position can remain filled, by *letter*.

In general then, for major constituents to be moved in a GWO language like English, grammatical machinery typically comes into play to ensure that a grammatical subject precedes the lexical verb. For major constituents to be moved in a PWO language like Spanish, little more than somewhat free reordering is often required.

The following excerpted passage was written by a Spanish-speaking native of Venezuela. What comments can you make about it that are relevant to the **typological** characteristics of English – e.g. SVO, GWO, obligatory subject, etc.?

[1]*In South America are many interesting place.* [2]*One of them is Carabobo Camp.*

[3]*Was here, in Carbobo, where the Independent War against Spain was won.*

[4]*Was a crude battle and many Latinoamericans were killed.* [5]*For any visitor is interesting to know that* [6]*in this place happened the liberty of Latinoamerica.*

[7]*Was Simon Bolívar the man who conduced the battle and* [8]*was him who got the liberty for four more countries.*

(continued)

ASSIGNMENT 117*   Null-Object: L2

There are cases in English where the **direct object** of a transitive verb is not present in the clause. Four such cases, two of which were displayed in previous assignments, would be the following:

> this hat which$_i$ I made t$_i$ for you (Assignment 49)
> This hat$_i$, I made t$_i$ for you (Assignment 34)
> I made Ø$_i$, and you wore Ø$_i$, this hat$_i$
> I made a hat$_i$ for you to wear Ø$_i$

In all such instances the apparent null-object is licensed by structural properties of the grammar. Disallowed in English, though not in many other languages, would be sentences like

> *I made the hat$_i$ and you wore Ø$_i$

One such language is Nepalese, which is typologically **topic-prominent**. In a study of the acquisition of English in adulthood by native speakers of Nepalese, Hartford (1995) gathered a sizable quantity of Nepalese/English IL data containing examples of otherwise disallowed **zero anaphora** such as the following, grouped into two sets:

(a) (i)   *I don't like to give you **my notes**$_i$. You may tear Ø$_i$ and make Ø$_i$ dirty.*

   (ii) *Oh friend where is **my umbrella**$_i$. Did you forget Ø$_i$? Please return Ø$_i$ as soon as possible.*

   (iii) *When I got **your invitation**$_i$ and put Ø$_i$ among books, then yesterday morning went in the market, ...*

   (iv) ***On this occasion**$_i$ the Nepalese soldiers observe Ø$_i$ by firing blank fires at the military parade ground.*

(continued)

(b) (i) [returning a defective video] *The sound is too bad to hear. Please give 0 a better one.*

(ii) [narrative folktale] *But the demons said that they [the sweets] had all fallen on the refuse-heaps and hence could not be touched by them [the demons]. So they$_i$ requested her to come down (from the tree) and give 0$_i$ the sweets herself.*

(iii) *People face their past differently. Mr. RS$_i$ has his own way$_j$. Why should we grudge 0$_i$ 0$_j$?*

(iv) *Further, the news item informs 0 that five day-care centres for the mentally retarded will be established.*

The researcher makes several observations concerning examples like these, one arising from facts of the discourse, the other concerning grammatical category. As for the discourse question, the null elements in one set can be analyzed as coreferential with the **topic**, whereas in the other set the null element refers to the discourse PARTICIPANTS and can easily be recovered from context. As for the grammar question, the null elements in the two sets represent different grammatical categories.

Briefly then:

1. For sets (a) and (b) and topic vs. discourse participant vis-à-vis the null element, which set displays which?

2. What grammatical category does the null element in (a) represent? What category in (b)?

SECTION D | Noun Phrase Accessibility Hierarchy (NAH)

<u>ASSIGNMENT</u> **The NAH (I)**
118*

The function of a **relative clause** (RC) is to modify a noun in the **main** or **matrix clause** (MC) in which the RC is embedded. The RC and MC therefore "share" the modified noun, in that the noun or its *wh-* referent is part of the internal structure of both clauses. Using again the examples of Assignment 49 plus some additional ones, notice the different grammatical positions that the relativized noun can occupy in the RC, where the bracketed labels designate the function of the moved *wh* element with relation to the rest of its clause; i.e. **SU** = subject, **DO** = direct object, **IO** = indirect object, **OBL** = oblique (also referred to by some as OPREP: object of a preposition), **GEN** = genitive, **OCOMP** = object of a comparative:

(a) *That's the person **who gave** me the book* [SU]

(b) *That's the book **which** I **gave** to the person* [DO]

(c) *That's the person **(to) whom** I **gave** the book* [IO]

(d) *That's the person **who(m)** the book is **about*** [OBL]

(e) *That's the person **whose book** I **borrowed*** [GEN]

(f) *That's the person **who(m)** you're **taller than*** [OCOMP]

These six positions in fact form a hierarchy, termed the **Noun Phrase Accessibility Hierarchy** or **NAH**, so named because of its distributional characteristics cross-linguistically. That is, if a language can relativize on a given NP position in the hierarchy, then it necessarily relativizes on all the higher positions, though not necessarily on a lower one. As is obvious, English relativizes on all six positions, a characteristic by no means shared by most of the world's languages.

(continued)

Name: _____   Date: __ / __ / __   Class: _____

For each of the sentences below, first put brackets around the relative clause, then state which of the six positions has been relativized upon. If a sentence does not contain a relative clause, simply write Ø. Note that identification of the relativized position is with reference to SURFACE STRUCTURE; e.g. the fact that in underlying structure the subject of a passive was in object position would be irrelevant here. Keep in mind that the categories in question are in reference to the **constituent** (i.e. relative) clause, not the **matrix** (i.e. main) clause.

1. *SU* . What does the guy [who has everything] expect to get?

2. ..... What do you give to the guy who has everything?

3. ..... That looks like a bed that's already been slept in.

4. ..... There are a lot of things that they just don't dare think about.

5. ..... I have interests outside my immediate work that I find satisfying.

6. ..... You learn a lot about authors you didn't know too much about to start with.

7. ..... Why is there all this stuff that we have to look up?

8. ..... That doesn't sound like the Ronald Reagan I remember talking to the crowds back in 1980.

9. ..... The candidate that they gave all that money is filing a claim that the money is tax-exempt.

10. ..... "The more I think about it, the more I think about guys passing me who I feel I'm a better hitter than." (RC headed by *who*: Los Angeles Times)

11. ..... What happened to the child whose school they paid all that money to?

12. ..... The idea that it's the other guy that should always pay is one I don't particularly like.

13. ..... The news that the team had won called for a celebration.

14. ..... The horse that lost the race that got a late start is owned by the syndicate.

ASSIGNMENT 119* The NAH (II)

Refer once more to the description of the Noun Phrase Accessibility Hierarchy (NAH) in the previous assignment. The following passage from a book published a few years ago is intended as an informal description of the hierarchy for the general reader:

> Nearly all languages have relative clauses ... but can deploy them in different circumstances according to a rigid, universally defined hierarchy ... In Malagasy ... only subjects can be modified by relative clauses ... In other languages subjects and direct objects may be modified by relative clauses but no other objects may be; in yet others, subjects, direct objects and indirect objects may be modified but objects of comparatives can not. (pp. 25–6)

The book's examples of such relativizing, drawn from English, are as follows:

A *man who likes women* is coming to dinner	[SUBJ]
I know a *man who likes women*	[DIR OBJ]
I gave it to the *man who likes women*	[INDIR OBJ]
Fred is taller than the *man who likes women*	[OBJ OF COMPAR]

Very briefly, what is fundamentally wrong with this depiction of the NAH?

ASSIGNMENT 120* The NAH and L2

Over the short history of second language acquisition as a research field, predictions have often been made as to degree of learning difficulty of the target language (TL) vis-à-vis the native language (NL). Some of these predictions were based upon perceived differences between the two languages that could be described in terms of markedness – for example, where nouns in the NL might be uninflected (unmarked) for plurality as opposed to inflection (marked) in the TL. These notions crystalized in what was termed the **Markedness Differential Hypothesis** or **MDH** (Eckman 1977: 321), which reads essentially as follows:

> The areas of difficulty that a language learner will have can be predicted on the basis of a systematic comparison of the grammars of the [N]ative [L]anguage [and] the [T]arget [L]anguage, . . . such that:
>
> (a) those areas of the [TL] which differ from the [NL] and are more marked than the [NL] will be difficult;
>
> (b) the relative degree of difficulty of the areas of the [TL] which are more marked than the [NL] will correspond to the relative degree of markedness;
>
> (c) those areas of the [TL] which are different from the [NL], but are not more marked than the [NL] will not be difficult.

Consider again the NAH and relative clause formation, as outlined in Assignment 118. The hierarchy, like all such hierarchies, can be taken as a statement of **markedness** relationships, such that the relativized positions in the hierarchy – SU > DO > IO > OBL > GEN > OCOMP – increase from top to bottom in degree of markedness. Think now about the acquisition of English L2 relative clauses. What single position in the NAH would the MDH suggest as having the most generalizability for extended learning of the other positions? In other words, which position is predicted to "get the most mileage" for learning purposes? Why?

SECTION E Implicationals

ASSIGNMENT 121* Implicational Universals

Implicational universals are of the form **if p then q**. Possible occurrences of p and/or q described by this principle would thus be the following:

p and   q

not-p and   q

not-p and not-q

Disallowed would be: **p and not-q**

The principle easily captures well-known facts such as that if a language has voiced word-final obstruents (corresponding to the p value above) then it also has – and in fact must have – voiceless word-final obstruents (the q value). By this principle then, if a language does NOT have word-final voiced obstruents, no prediction can be made as to whether that language has voiceless word-final obstruents: it may or it may not.

The principle also captures the relationships obtaining between members of a hierarchy such as the NAH (see Section D). In the words of Hawkins (1991: 477–8), where the hierarchy is conceived as having four positions,

> if a language has a primary relativization strategy operating on oblique NPs [OBL], then that strategy will operate on indirect objects [IO]; and if it operates on indirect objects, it will operate on direct objects [DO]; and if it operates on direct objects, it will operate on subjects [SU].

Using the values p (= OBL), q (= IO), r (= DO), and s (= SU), plot the five possible combinations of these four values in hierarchical fashion. Use "not" for the negative value.

1.   p   and   q   and   r   and   s
2.
3.
4.
5.

ASSIGNMENT 122* Implicational Universals: L1/L2

As already noted from the previous assignment, the possible/impossible realizations of implicational universals of the form **if p then q** are: **p & q / not-p & q / not-p & not-q / *p & not-q**. Language learning predictions based on implicationals have been made for both L1 and L2 (Hawkins 1991) and a number of studies have been conducted over the years that largely bear out such predictions, some of these concerning the ORDER in which given entities are acquired.

With reference only to the p/q formulation, what two possible – and one impossible – routes of acquisition for p and q are predicted to occur therein? Assume that at the start neither p nor q is present (not-p & not-q) and that at the end both are present (p & q). In plotting the acquisition routes, change one of the values at a time or both values, bearing in mind that the implicational statement also allows SIMULTANEOUS acquisition for p/q.

1. possible:
   not-p & not-q   →

2. possible:
   not-p & not-q   →

3. NOT possible:
   *not-p & not-q   →

ASSIGNMENT 123** Implicationals and the NAH: L2

It was noted in Assignment 121 that the **Noun Phrase Accessibility Hierarchy (NAH)** can be viewed as a set of **implicational** relationships for grammatical positions upon which a given language can relativize, again those positions being SU > DO > IO > OBL > GEN > OCOMP. It is also possible, using the implicational formulation, to make additional precise statements – i.e. facts about distribution, predictions for acquisition – that derive from the NAH.

Using your best guess, formulate **if p then q** statements for each of the following (where p corresponds to lower on the hierarchy and q corresponds to higher):

1. positions of relativization (distribution)
    If a language *can relativize on position X, then it can relativize on position X—n*

2. frequency of occurrence (distribution)
    If a language ...

    . . . .

3. resumptive pronouns in relativized positions (distribution) (See Assignment 55)
    If a language ...

    . . . .

4. resumptive pronouns (acquisition)
    If a learner ...

    . . . .

5. production and comprehension (acquisition)
    If a learner ...

    . . . .

6. relative pronoun substitution (acquisition)
    If a learner ...

    . . . .

ASSIGNMENT 124** Implicationals and the MUP

Recall from the assignments in Section C the discussion of the allowance in some languages of so-called **null-subjects** – i.e. **pro-drop** languages. It has been noted in some of the recent research literature that there appears to be a correlation between a language's licensing of null-subjects and its verb inflection. The correlation has assumed the form of a principle – namely, the **Morphological Uniformity Principle**, or **MUP**. The MUP states (in informal terms) that a language can have null-subjects if and only if its verb inflection is morphologically uniform, where "uniform" is defined as inflection (a) either on all verb forms within a paradigm or (b) on none of them. The (a) option would apply, for example, to Spanish, the (b) option to Chinese. A good example of a language that is not morphologically uniform and therefore does not license null subjects is English. Note that the principle is formulated in such a way as to allow the possibility that a language may be morphologically uniform but still not permit null-subjects. German is such a language.

The effects of the MUP can thus be exemplified by the four languages just cited in the following way:

SPANISH/CHINESE	GERMAN	ENGLISH
+ uniform	+ uniform	− uniform
+ null-subject	− null-subject	− null-subject

With reference to these facts, recast the MUP as an implicational universal – i.e. **if p then q** – and represent the four combinations of p and q along with the corresponding choice of values among [± uniform] and [± null-subject]. State the implicational universal in the form that reflects the fact that [± null-subject] is an EFFECT of the MUP rather than the other way around.

If . . . . ,

then . . . .

p [	] and	q [	]
not-p [	] and	q [	]
not-p [	] and	not-q [	]
*p [	] and	not-q [	]

ASSIGNMENT 125* Implicationals and the MUP: L1

Recall from Assignment 123 that implicational universals are claimed to be statements, among other things, of ordering in **language acquisition**. With reference to the implicational formulation concerning the MUP from the previous assignment, state a prediction of the orders – two possible and one impossible – in which [± **null-subject**] and [± **uniformity**] will be manifested in the language of a child in the early stages of the acquisition of English.

1. possible:
   [+ null-subject] & [+ uniformity] $\longrightarrow$

2. possible:
   [+ null-subject] & [+ uniformity] $\longrightarrow$

3. NOT possible:
   [+ null-subject] & [+ uniformity] $\longrightarrow$

   Note that the above implicational statements have taken [+ null-subject]/ [+ uniformity] to be the child's initial state. What problems would arise if the child were to start out assuming that the language he was learning is [– uniform]?

ASSIGNMENT 126** Implicationals and Pronouns/Anaphors: L1/L2

Implicational universals, as already noted in the previous assignments, are of the form **if p then q** and typically capture the relationships obtaining between members of a hierarchy such as the NAH (Section D). Another such hierarchy (cf. Comrie 1990) is described by the distribution cross-linguistically of the morphological representations, within single languages, of **object pronouns** and **reflexive pronouns** (i.e. **anaphors**). For example, some languages distinguish pronouns and anaphors morphologically for all three persons (1st, 2nd, and 3rd). English – with *me/myself, you/yourself, him/himself* – is such a language. Some languages make the distinction only for 3rd person; the Romance languages are good examples of this (e.g. French: *me/me, te/te,* but *le/se*). And some languages do not draw the distinction morphologically at all; Old English is such an example.

1. How would these observations be represented in terms of an **implicational universal**? That is, what would be the values assigned to p and q in this instance?

2. With regard to implicationals and the above examples, can you think of a possible reason WHY there should be such a hierarchy – an explanation that appeals to the real-world situation obtaining between interlocutors in a communicative setting?

(continued)

3.   Suppose it were newly discovered that some language in the world hap-
     pened to violate this particular implicational universal – i.e. suppose some
     language showed a pattern of morphological distinction for 1st person pro-
     nouns/anaphors but not 2nd or 3rd person. Is there any reason to think that
     the pronoun/anaphor system in the language which shows the violation
     would be any harder to learn than the systems in those languages which do
     not? Why, or why not?

PART V

Other Areas

SECTION A Form and Function

ASSIGNMENT 127* Function-Filling Forms

English abounds in constructions that are the result of movement of some kind and such constructions formed the bulk of the material in Part II, with a handy inventory of traditionally the most common ones displayed in Assignment 34. Many of those, and especially those involving **extraposition,** are contextualized in the following passage:

1 *Although one can hear talk of a settlement, it is not easy*
2 *to see how any real breakthrough can occur in negotiations in*
3 *the near future. However, Washington continues to be*
4 *encouraged by the seeming willingness by the Russians to*
5 *discuss troop levels in the second stage of negotiations.*
6 *That talks are actually going on is the most encouraging sign*
7 *of all.*
8 *Diplomats with long experience consider it natural then*
9 *to be skeptical in such situations. It is the newcomer to*
10 *government who tends to be optimistic. Nevertheless, what*
11 *mainly seems to interest the Russians is helping to build a*
12 *positive atmosphere for Senate consideration of the impending*
13 *new Strategic Arms Limitation agreement. Without this there*
14 *may soon come a time when one will wonder what sort of*
15 *atmosphere it would have to be that could help divert NATO*
16 *from its current arms modernization program. Only now,*
17 *however, do we have the luxury of a choice. And as long as*
18 *there appears to be a choice, then choose we must.*

(continued)

Name: _____ Date: __ / __ / __ Class: _____

Scan the above passage and find and list one example of each of the constructions cited below. All of them, as already mentioned, were first introduced in Assignment 34. Other assignments in which there was further elaboration and/or discussion are indicated. **Extraposition** is abbreviated as **EXTRA**. Note that there are two occurrences of the construction for nos. 1 and 12, three for no. 11.

1. topicalization: . . . .
    . . . .

2. **wh-movement without I-movement** (Assignment 39): . . . .
    . . . .

3. **I-movement** (Assignment 35): . . . .
    . . . .

4. **cleft sentence** (Assignment 52): . . . .
    . . . .

5. **pseudo-cleft sentence:** . . . .
    . . . .

6. **clausal subject (without EXTRA):** . . . .
    . . . .

7. **clausal subject (EXTRA):** . . . .
    . . . .

8. **relative clause (EXTRA):** . . . .
    . . . .

9. **noun complement (EXTRA)** (Assignment 52): . . . .
    . . . .

10. **clausal object (EXTRA):** . . . .
    . . . .

11. **raising-verb clause** (Assignments 45, 46): . . . .
    . . . .
    . . . .

12. **existential clause:** . . . .
    . . . .

13. **passive** (Assignment 66): . . . .
    . . . .

ASSIGNMENT 128* Function and Passive: L1/L2

Among the various forms appearing in the text displayed in the previous assignment is one example of the **passive**:

> *However, Washington continues to **be encouraged** by the seeming willingness of the Russians to discuss troop levels in the second stage of negotiations.*

Use of the passive here licenses, to the right of the verb, a **by-phrase (PP)** of new and salient information. To choose the **active** here instead would force all this material into subject position and thereby greatly disrupt the flow of discourse.

Although the passive may serve functions even beyond satisfactory arrangement of old and new information (cf. Assignment 132), it is still assumed by many that passive and active are interchangeable. That this assumption is erroneous was well demonstrated a few years back in a piece of L2 acquisition research examining the phenomenon of L2 "avoidance." As a prelude to comparing the use of the English passive by native speakers with that by Hebrew–English bilinguals, Seliger (1989) asked a group of native-speaker linguistics students (the number was unspecified) to write from three to ten sentences on each of the following topics:

(a) how paper is made
(b) how an omelet is made
(c) how a baby is diapered
(d) how milk is processed
(e) how a candle is made
(f) how ice cubes are made
(g) how teeth are brushed
(h) how mail is sent and delivered

Although there had been a claim, based on a small amount of prior psycholinguistic research, that questions in the passive would elicit the passive in answers as well, the results of Seliger's study challenged this. It turned out that passives abounded in the writing on topics (a), (d), (e), and (h), whereas they were almost totally absent for topics (b), (c), (f), and (g). Typical of the writing where passives proliferated was the following:

(continued)

(a) **how paper is made**: *Trees are cut down and taken to a paper mill. Here they are cleaned and processed. Various types of paper were made.*

Typical of the writing where passives did not appear was the following:

(b) **how an omelet is made**: *The first thing you do is to put some butter in the frying pan. Turn the stove on to a low flame. While the butter is melting, crack an egg and put it in the frying pan. Make sure the flame isn't too high.*

There would clearly seem to be a pattern then in whether passive or active is chosen in writing on these topics. The conclusion of the researcher, based on these findings, is that use of the passive by native speakers (at least when describing procedures like the above) is determined by the topic chosen.

Briefly, what is it about the topics in (a), (d), (e), and (h), as distinct from (b), (c), (f), and (g), that appears to be associated with selection of the passive? Or in other words, what **language function** is the passive serving in these instances?

After obtaining the data described above, Seliger (1989) ran an experiment to compare oral performance on use of the passive by six native speakers with that of six Hebrew–English bilinguals. It had already been determined that the bilinguals knew and could use the English passive CONSTRUCTION and that Hebrew also has a structurally similar passive, though its use is rare. The task was the same as that above, calling for oral description of (a) how an omelet is made, (b) how a baby is diapered, (c) how oranges are picked and sent to the market, and (d) how mail is sent and delivered. The prediction was that native-speaker choice of passive would be topic-dependent, as above – i.e. appearing in answers to (a) and (b), absent in (c) and (d) – whereas the passive would not be used at all by the bilinguals. The test subjects performed as predicted.

In conducting this bit of research, Seliger wanted to probe more seriously the loosely defined notion of L2 "avoidance," as already mentioned. In his words, "nonuse of target structures can result from differences between L1 and L2, ignorance, non-acquisition or presystematic use of the not yet fully acquired form, or from true avoidance" (1989: 32). Therefore, if the six Hebrew–English bilinguals exhibited "true avoidance" in this experiment, what is it about the passive that was "truly avoided"?

ASSIGNMENT 129* Discontinuous Dependency

Assignment 34 presented a battery of constructions in which informal rules of various kinds served to move constituents either to the left – **fronting** – or to the right – **backing**. As noted there, one sub-class of backing constructions comes about through the process of **extraposition** and the creation of a **discontinuous dependency**, and a few examples of this were encountered in Assignment 127. Repeated here for convenience is the inventory of extraposition examples from Assignment 34, together with the version of each in which no extraposition has applied, for purposes of comparison.

Extraposition of:

clausal subject:	*It's good **that she writes***
	(*That she writes* is good)
clausal object:	*I consider **it** good **that she writes***
	(I consider *that she writes* good)
relative clause:	**the things** *I mentioned **that she writes***
	(the things *that she writes* [that] I mentioned)
noun complement:	*What **evidence** is there **that she writes?***
	(What evidence *that she writes* is there?)
adjective complement:	*How **likely** is she **to write?***)
	(How likely *to write* is she?)

Consideration will be given in the next assignment as to why the discontinuity is generally preferred here over the alternative without it.

(continued)

The following sentences all contain examples of extraposition, resulting in each case in a discontinuous dependency. Put a circle around the construction that has been extraposed and draw a line from the circle to the position in the sentence from which the movement took place. Think about why most of these versions WITHOUT extraposition sound awkward. Is there anything unusual about nos. 9 and 10? Finally, note that one of the examples contains TWO, interlocking, discontinuities, where extraposition has applied twice.

For example:

A rumor circulated (that he was a spy.)

1. A man came in who was wearing a very funny hat.

. . . .

2. Did you do that yourself?

. . . .

3. The time had come to address the issue.

. . . .

4. The problem arose of what to do about it.

. . . .

5. We looked some information up that was crucial for them.

. . . .

6. A committee has been formed consisting of X, Y, and Z.

. . . .

7. What business is it of yours?

. . . .

8. All of us were upset but you.

. . . .

9. That's a different situation from the one you just brought up.

. . . .

10. I think there's another contributing factor to this difficulty.

. . . .

Which sentence contains the **interlocking** dependencies?   No. . . . . . .

ASSIGNMENT 130* Theme and Rheme

Consider again the first sentence in the exercise section from the previous assignment:

(a) *A man   came in [who was wearing a very funny hat]*
      |_____↑

As already noted, (a) contains a discontinuity brought about by separation – i.e. **extraposition** – of the relative clause *who was wearing a funny hat* from the subject NP *a man* with which it forms a constituent. Yet most people would agree that sentence (a) WITH extratraposition sounds somewhat better, even devoid of context, than it does WITHOUT, as in (b):

(b) *A man [who was wearing a very funny hat] came in*

What happens then if the content is switched between main clause and relative clause – that is, if the main clause is made the relative clause and vice versa? We would then have version (c), which again sounds reasonable enough:

(c) *A man [who came in] was wearing a very funny hat*

But notice what happens if the relative clause is now **extraposed**, as was the case in (a); the result is (d):

(d) *?A man   was wearing a very funny hat [who came in]*
      |_____↑

   To most ears, (d) sounds extremely awkward and it is useful to consider the possible reason for this. Look first at the information conveyed by the subject in (a) and (b) – namely, that of a man wearing a very funny hat – and by the predicate – namely, that of the action of coming in. To most ears, the subject would seem to have more force, more weight, more prominence, more salience than the predicate. It is as if the order of the two should perhaps be reversed. Indeed, in languages in which word order is freer than in English (e.g. Italian,
                                                                    (continued)

333

Spanish, etc.), it is precisely the reverse order (ungrammatical in English) that one would often see for the arrangement of the above sentence content, something like (e):

(e)   *Came in a man who was wearing a very funny hat.*

In terms of the relative prominence of the two halves of the sentence then, it is the LESS prominent that naturally occurs early and the MORE prominent late. Figuring in degree of prominence are said to be two factors, one informational, the other structural (Quirk et al. 1985). In (a) the prominence of *who was wearing a very funny hat* relative to *came in* comes about via the quantity and importance of information conveyed and via the weight and complexity of the structures deployed. The terms given to "less/more prominent" from an informational perspective are **theme** and **rheme**, respectively, and the natural placement of **rhematic** material toward the end of the sentence – e.g. the relative clause in (a), the VP in (c) – is called **end focus**. From a structural standpoint, the "heavier" and more complex material also finds its natural location to be toward the end of the sentence – e.g. again the relative clause in (a), the VP in (c); hence the reference to **end weight**. These two forces most often work in tandem as in the above, though we shall later see what happens when they occasionally conflict.

Not surprisingly then, it is the subject that is most likely to carry **thematic** material, the predicate **rhematic** material, though it is well to remember that these are tendencies, not absolutes. The feeling of "movement" within a sentence from theme to rheme is said to represent its **communicative dynamism** or **CD**. Extraposition **form** in (a) then (as well as in the examples from the previous assignment) serves the dual **function** of ordering theme before rheme (end focus) and shifting heavier material to the right (end weight).

Taking into consideration the above observations concerning theme/rheme, end focus/weight, and CD, explain very briefly why the extraposition in example (d), though perfectly grammatical in a strictly formal sense, seems so awkward.

Existentials, Definiteness, and Theme/Rheme: L2

Many sentences like those listed below have been documented in research on English IL produced by Mandarin speakers. It has often been assumed that such sentences represent malformed relative clauses, the result of transfer of the "serial verb" construction from Mandarin – i.e. "a sentence that contains two or more verb phrases or clauses juxtaposed without any marker indicating what relationship is between them" (Li and Thompson 1981: 594). Considering that sentence-initial NPs in Mandarin are automatically interpreted as definite and noting that all the examples below have a sentence-initial **existential**, what equally plausible analysis might one adopt in the context of **definiteness/ indefiniteness** and **theme/rheme?**

(a) *There's a lot of people find their husband or wife in parties.*

(b) *In a coeducational school, there are many students have this good opportunity.*

(c) *There are a small amount of people get married in their teenage.*

(d) *There were a lot of events happen in my country.*

(e) *There are so many original Taiwan people live around the lake.*

ASSIGNMENT **Given and New**
132*

The previous two assignments have been concerned with form/function relations demonstrated through introduction of the concepts of **theme** and **rheme, end focus** and **end weight,** and **communicative dynamism.** These all have largely to do with language form in the service of language function WITHIN THE SENTENCE; when or where a language construct is likely to be **extraposed** served as an excellent example of this. What happens, however, when the form/function question is lifted BEYOND THE SENTENCE? For the following display, a short stretch of English technical writing has been arranged in such a way that the middle sentence appears in three different versions, all grammatical, all expressing the same content, but NOT all of equal appropriateness:

Weathering and erosion of rock exposed to the atmosphere constantly remove particles from the rock ...

(1)

They call these rock particles sediment ...	*Sediment is what these rock particles are called ...*	*These rock particles are called sediment ...*
(2a)	(2b)	(2c)

As sediments accumulate, the upper layers press down on the lower ones.

(3)

One of the three versions (2a–c) would seem to form a "best fit" for linking the two outer sentences (1) and (2) in creating an appropriately smooth text, and for most speakers that version is (2c). What is it then about the arrangement of content and choice of syntax in (2c) that makes that version feel more natural than the others? Or to frame the question in terms of the form/function theme being developed in this section, what language function is being served by what language form(s) in (2c) and not in (2a) or (2b)?

In arriving at an answer to this question, one needs to look more directly at the semantic content of the sentence in question. The essence of content for (2a–c) in lexical terms can be thought of as the notion of "rock particle," the notion of "sediment," and the event of "calling." If we lay this content out in

(continued)

skeletal fashion and in the order in which it appears in the text, we will have the following:

| rock particles (1) | call (2a) : rock particles : sediment | sediment (3) |

| rock particles (1) | sediment (2b) : rock particles : call | sediment (3) |

| rock particles (1) | rock particles (2c) : call : sediment | sediment (3) |

Source: adapted from a convention utilized by Gleason (1965); content from Rutherford (1977)

It is not hard to see that the link between (1) and (3) afforded by (2c), and not by (2a–b), comes about through placing *rock particles* earliest in the sentence and *sediment* last. *Rock particles*, by virtue of its having already been introduced in the discourse represented by (1), is said to be **given** information in (2c). On the other hand, newly introduced into that part of the discourse represented in (2) is *sediment*, which thereby constitutes **new** information. The placement of the **given** early and the **new** late, observed in (2c) and not in (2a–b), is what has achieved the desirable smooth transition.

Arrangement of sentence elements to satisfy what has been termed the **given–new principle** often relies crucially upon syntactic devices many of which were earlier encountered in their more formal aspects. Thus, placement of *rock particles* first and *sediment* last in (2c) forces the use of the **passive** (Assignment 66). Leaving these two NPs in their original positions, as in (az), is less satisfactory in that **thematic** *rock particles* does not occur early. Use of the **pseudo-cleft** construction (Assignment 34) plus inversion in (2a), where *sediment* occurs early and *rock particles* relatively late, runs afoul of the given–new principle.

(continued)

Each of the following is conceived as a mini-discourse in which the skeletal sentence in brackets is intended to follow naturally from what precedes. Write the bracketed material as a full sentence, changing the order of constituents, where necessary or appropriate, in observance of the given–new principle. Where **end focus** and **end weight** (see Assignment 130) come into conflict in no. 9, which one wins out?

1. A: *What shall we call him?*   B: *Fafnir.*
   A: [find funny – that name – most people]

   A: *That name most people would find funny* . . . .

2. *Place a small amount of sulfur in a test tube about half full of carbon tetrachloride (CCL4).*
   [[NEG] should breathe under any circumstances – the CCL4 vapors]

   . . . .

3. A: *What's an easy experiment to perform?*
   B: [easy – [demonstrate – [The earth has gravity]]]

   . . . .

4. A: *Is it hard to demonstrate that the **moon** has gravity?*
   B: No. [easy – [demonstrate – that]] too

   . . . .

5. *Another five bodies have bene washed up on shore,*
   [bring – the total number of recorded casualties – to 23]

   . . . .

6. *Air coming up from the lungs causes the vocal chords to vibrate.*
   [stretch across the larynx – the vocal chords]

   . . . .

7. *The upper part of the respiratory tract is called the larynx.*
   [stretch across the larynx – the vocal chords]

   . . . .

8. *Several scientists are beginning to reconsider the experiment planned for next month.*
   [[It might not work] – be – their opinion at the moment]

   . . . .

9. *Several scientists are of the opinion that next moth's planned experiment may not be successful*
   [[It might not work] – be – Dr Weiss's opinion also]

   . . . .

ASSIGNMENT **Given and New:**
133* **Expository Prose**

Fleshing out of the skeletal sentences in the previous assignment was designed to create mini-discourses. No. 7 is a case in point, where the rendition with **inversion** seems decidedly preferable to that without it:

(*The upper part of the respiratory tract is called the larynx.*)
Stretching across the larynx are the vocal chords.
?The vocal chords stretch across the larynx.

The larynx is **given** information and the one construction that can serve here to locate it near the beginning of the sentence, its natural position, is that of **inversion**.

In an earlier very detailed study, Green (1980) documented a variety of functions that inversion may serve, the one in the example above where the given–new principle comes into play being that of "connection." Green (1980: 588) offers the following literary examples of such connection drawn from the work of S.J. Perelman, James Thurber, Brendan Gill, and Leo Rosten:

(1) *This is called the New York Marble Cemetery, and a block away, open to the view of the passerby, is another known by the same name, the most tranquil cemetery in town to look upon, probably.*

(2) [Hellcat fighter plane mentioned in preceding sentence]
Holding the stick of this four-hundred-mile-an-hour ship is a small firm hand.

(3) [Opinions about marriage in another culture described in preceding paragraphs]
In so emphatic, consistent, and homogeneous a consensus was born the useful, if quixotic institution of the professional matchmaker.

(4) [Topic of preceding sentence is a new driver's license]
Attached to it, as always, is an application blank for next year's license.

(5) [Topic of preceding sentence is an auction room at Park Bernet]
Stacked on shelves were hundreds of cast-iron horses, wagons, fire engines, banks, tin clowns, doll houses, carousels, miniature railways, and so on ad infinitum.

(continued)

For many, it is hard to imagine how the above examples of expository prose could have been written WITHOUT inversion. For an understanding of this, try rewriting each of the five in original subject–predicate order:

1. . . . .
. . . .

2. . . . .
. . . .

3. . . . .
. . . .

4. . . . .
. . . .

5. . . . .
. . . .
. . . .

Aside from contravention of the given–new principle, can you identify anything else in your rewritten examples that would make them more difficult to comprehend by the average reader?

ASSIGNMENT 134* Given and New: L2

Satisfaction of the **given–new principle** in the previous assignment was achieved by means of a variety of different syntactic constructions – e.g. topicalization, extraposition, raising, and so on. Two more constructions that are widely assumed often to facilitate the arrangement of given and new are **cleft sentence** (see Assignment 52) and **pseudo-cleft sentence**. Examples of these drawn from Assignment 34 were the following:

- **cleft:** *It's Mary who writes* (cf. Mary writes)

- **pseudo-cleft**: *What Mary does is write* (cf. Mary writes)

In the cleft example, there is a **presupposition** that someone writes and an **assertion** that that someone is "Mary." In the pseudo-cleft example, there is a presupposition that Mary does something and an assertion that that something is "write." There is thus a focus on the assertion, achieved for clefting with intonation as well, and the two are often labeled **focus** constructions.

The assumed link-up between **given** and **presupposed, new** and **asserted,** figured in an early empirical study (Carrell 1978) of sensitivity to the given–new principle in English by 145 non-native-speaking adults. The constructions chosen for the one test instrument used – a 28-item questionnaire – were exclusively the **cleft** and **pseudo-cleft**. The verbs selected were transitive, thus facilitating (pseudo-)clefting on either of two NPs: subject or object. In the words of the researcher, "the inter-relationships among these two types of cleft and pseudo-cleft structures make them an ideal paradigm for testing the difference between given and new information" (Carrell 1978: 235), and it should be emphasized that this study was the first of its kind. The results of the test supported the hypothesis – namely, that L2 learner responses would reveal sensitivity to the given–new principle. No data were presented, however, that separate the clefting responses from the pseudo-clefting; the two were treated together. We will presently return to this.

Examples of each type of question (four) used in the test follow here. For each of the four, circle the (i) or (ii) response, whichever you think is the more appropriate, then answer the questions below.

(continued)

Name: _____   Date: __ / __ / __   Class: _____

(a) *What is the cat chasing?*
   (i)   *It is the rat that the cat is chasing.*
   (ii) *It is the cat that is chasing the rat.*

(b) *What is chasing the rat?*
   (i)   *It is the rat that the cat is chasing.*
   (ii) *It is the cat that is chasing the rat.*

(c) *What is the cow eating?*
   (i)   *What the cow is eating is grass.*
   (ii) *What is eating grass is the cow.*

(d) *What is eating grass?*
   (i)   *What the cow is eating is grass.*
   (ii) *What is eating grass is the cow.*

Consider again what is being tested here and the appropriateness of the test instrument:

1. Apart from the given–new issue, are sentences with clefting and pseudo-clefting likely to be the form of the most natural response to questions like those presented? Why, or why not?

2. Do the cleft answers sound any more or less natural than the pseudo-cleft? If there is a difference, what might account for it? Think in terms of the FORMAL relationship of the question to the answer and the arrangement of sentence content.

3. What bearing, if any, does all this have on the claim that L2 learners show sensitivity to the given–new principle?

Pragmatics: Illocution and Clause Type

Many linguists work in the realm of what is termed **pragmatics**, or the relationship between what an utterance means in and of itself and what a speaker means by uttering it – namely, the **speech act**. The speech act can be regarded as embracing three subsidiary acts, as noted by Levinson (1983: 236) and Leech (1983: 199) and drawn from the work of the philosopher J.L. Austin:

locutionary act: the utterance of a sentence with determinate sense and reference
i.e. s(peaker) says to h(earer) that X

illocutionary act: the making of an assertion, offer, promise, etc., in uttering a sentence, by virtue of the conventional FORCE associated with it
e.g. In saying X, s ASSERTS that P

perlocutionary act: the bringing about of effects on the audience by means of uttering the sentence
e.g. By saying X, s CONVINCES h that P

Here we shall be concerned primarily with the **illocutionary** part of this picture, a sample of the kinds of illocutionary force that an utterance may convey being the discourse functions of questioning, stating, promising, warning, requesting, exclaiming, announcing, ordering, congratulating, thanking, etc.

Linguists have traditionally classified the sentence or clause into four basic structural types – **declarative, interrogative, exclamative, imperative** – each closely paired with its TYPICAL discourse function, drawn from the above and having the illocutionary force of **statement, question, exclamation, directive**, respectively.

(continued)

For each of the utterances below, indicate its **clause type (CT)** and what you believe could be its **illocutionary force (IF)**, given appropriate context. Be careful not to confuse IF with **perlocutionary force** (e.g. persuading, dissuading, impressing, deceiving, insulting, flattering, etc.). Finally, supply appropriate punctuation.

1. *Would you mind handing me that screwdriver*

    CT: *interrogative* . . . . IF: *requesting* . . . .

2. *Look out*

    CT: . . . . IF: . . . .

3. *Where is it written in the sky that people should own guns*

    CT: . . . . IF: . . . .

4. *Boy, did she do a terrific job or what*

    CT: . . . . IF: . . . .

5. *I wonder whether that's the right thing to do*

    CT: . . . . IF: . . . .

6. *I don't promise to be there for every session*

    CT: . . . . IF: . . . .

7. *I promise not to be there for every session*

    CT: . . . . IF: . . . .

8. *Since when do we have to pay money for this*

    CT: . . . . IF: . . . .

9. *Lemme tell you, that's some kind of kitchen*

    CT: . . . . IF: . . . .

10. *What big teeth you have*

    CT: . . . . IF: . . . .

ASSIGNMENT 136* **Pragmatics: Queclaratives**

Consider sentence no. 3 from the previous assignment:

Where is it written in the sky that people should own guns?

As already noted, the **clause type** represented here is **interrogative**. The **illocutionary force** of the (contextless) preferred reading of the sentence, however, is not that of a question but of a **statement**, in this case a negative one, something like "It is not written in the sky that people should own guns" (itself tantamount to saying that people should NOT own guns). A sentence of this kind, with clause type interrogative/question but the illocutionary force of a statement/declarative, has been aptly labeled with an amalgamation of two of these terms: que[stion/de]clarative) – **queclarative** (Sadock 1971). Note, however, that sentences of this kind would seem often to be ambiguous. That is, in the (albeit unlikely) event that another person had just uttered the sentence *It is written in the sky that people should own guns,* then the reading for the above example as an appropriate response would have to be that of a straight question (and containing the presupposition that people should own guns).

Although some of the sentences listed below can be interpreted ambiguously (i.e. as both queclarative and straight question), some cannot. For each sentence, check "yes" or "no" – with "yes" if it is possible at all to get an ambiguous reading, even with effort. Do the unambiguous items fall consistently into one category (queclarative, straight question)? Finally, consider what might make an ambiguous interpretation of the "no" items actually impossible.

(continued)

Name: _____ Date: __/__/__ Class: _____

		Ambiguous?	
		Yes	No
1.	*Who cares?*	...	...
2.	*Does anybody care?*	...	...
3.	*Who the hell cares?*	...	...
4.	*Do phonemes have anything to do with language?*	...	...
5.	*Do phonemes have a damn thing to do with language?*	...	...
6.	*Who says so?*	...	...
7.	*Says who?*	...	...
8.	*What's she done for me?*	...	...
9.	*What's she ever done for me?*	...	...
10.	*Can I help it if they don't like it?*	...	...
11.	*Since when have we had to ask permission?*	...	...
12.	*Since when do we have to ask permission?*	...	...

<u>ASSIGNMENT</u> **Pragmatics:**

137*   **Queclaratives: L2**

It is well known that in the acquisition of correct wh-question form, adult learners of L2 English pass through an early stage of development in which wh-fronting occurs without I-movement (subject–AUX inversion) – e.g. *What he said* for *What did he say* (Assignment 39). In a study of the acquisition of English wh-question form by adult French speakers, Bialystok (1983) found, among other things, that there was a dramatic difference in rate of accuracy between intermediate and advanced stages when wh-question FUNCTION was taken into account. That is, at the intermediate stage learner questions often took the following form (where the actual errors are hypothetical, however, since none were cited in the article):

What she should do in that situation? [opinion]
What he did then? [information]
What that means? [clarification]
Why she SHOULD *have an abortion?* [queclarative]

At the advanced stage, learner questions would take the following form (again with hypothetical data):

What should she do in that situation?
What did he do then?
What does that mean?
Why she SHOULD *have an abortion?*

On the basis of the above data, what comment could be made about acquisition of I-movement (i.e. Subject–AUX inversion) vis-à-vis the **form** and **function** of wh-questions?

ASSIGNMENT **Pragmatics vs.**
138* **Ergativity: L1**

Recall from Assignment 71 the characteristics of unaccusativity and the class
of constructions containing a verb identified as **ergative**. Comrie (1987) observes
that **syntactic ergativity** can be seen in a comparison of two sentences such as
(a) and (b) below, with regard to the relation between the understood subject
of the infinitive (i.e. PRO in generative terms) and its coreference. Think in
terms of the antecedent controling interpretation of the subject of the infinitive
and the relation of that controller to its verb (*want* or *tell*):

(a)   *I want to leave now*

(b)   *Harry told me to leave now*

Although ergativity is cited as a general formal property of subordinate clauses
realized as infinitives such as those in (a) and (b), Comrie notes that the property
is superseded by pragmatic considerations in an example like (c):

(c)   *Harry promised me to leave now*

   Briefly, in what way can the syntactic relations in (a) and (b) be perceived
from the standpoint of syntactic ergativity and how do pragmatic/semantic factors over-ride in (c)?

   It has been noted (C. Chomsky, 1969) that young children's earliest interpretation of sentences like (c) is one in which the strict syntactic reading holds;
in other words, the pragmatic/semantic factor does NOT over-ride. What then
would be a plausible paraphrase for (c) corresponding to how this sentence
would be understood by a young child?

SECTION B   Deixis and Iconicity

ASSIGNMENT 139* **Deixis: Temporal**

Consider the matter of pragmatic appropriateness concerning the expression of time in the following sentences:

On December 8 President Roosevelt said to the American people ...

(a) ... *"Yesterday, Pearl Harbor was bombed"*

(b) ? ... *that* **yesterday,** *Pearl Harbor was/had been bombed*

(c) ... *that* **the day before,** *Pearl Harbor had been bombed*

Although (a) and (c) are the kind of sentence that might easily be found in a history text, (b) is not. *Yesterday* in (b) refers not to the day before December 8 (i.e. December 7) but to the day before that particular sentence was uttered; unless (b) was actually UTTERED on December 8, the sentence is therefore pragmatically inappropriate. Thus two different time frames are at issue here: one of them is the time of uttering, termed **coding time;** the other is the time of the event referred to in the utterance, termed **reference time.** The proper interpretation of *yesterday* can only be with respect to coding time.

   Similar features are to be found in the use of expressions of location and direction, such as

(d) **Come** *over* **here** *on your new bicycle*

(e) **Go** *over* **there** *on your new bicycle*

where *come* and *here* in (d) are generally interpretable in reference to motion **toward the location of the speaker,** *go* and *there* in (e) **away from speaker location.** (Refinements of this are to be seen in Assignment 142.)

   Interpretation of an expression that is tied to the time and place of its utterance is termed **deixis,** from the Greek word meaning "to point." Deictic characteristics range well beyond these examples, however, to embrace for instance **person deixis,** as in the use of the personal pronouns, **discourse deixis,** as in the use of *this* and *that* in discourse reference, **social deixis,** as in the encoding of social relationships among interlocutors, etc. The material in this section is concerned primarily with **time deixis** and **place deixis.**

(continued)

All of the time expressions in the following list can be interpreted deictically, whereas some can be interpreted non-deictically as well. For each one, indicate whether it is **deictic (D)** or both **deictic and non-deictic (D/ND)**. For those that can be interpreted only as D, write what the non-deictic COUNTERPART could be. For example:

		Non-deictic counterpart
early	D/ND	
yesterday	D	*the day before*
1. *from now on*		
2. *recently*		
3. *a second ago*		
4. *in a while*		
5. *this day → today*		
6. *tomorrow*		
7. *henceforth*		
8. *just now*		
9. *next/last*		
10. *this night → tonight*		
11. *last night*		
12. *this week/month/year/century*		
13. *this July/Thursday*		
14. *after awhile*		
15. *this morning*		
16. *in an hour*		
17. *soon*		
18. *right now*		
19. *yesterday evening*		
20. *later*		

ASSIGNMENT 140* Temporal and Spatial Reference

It is well known that many single lexical items can serve to establish **temporal** as well as **spatial** reference, either deictic or non-deictic. For example, the preposition *at* occurs in both *at noon* (temporal) and *at home* (spatial).

For each of the items below (some represented as pairs), compose two simple NPs (DPs) as complements of that item, one exemplifying temporal reference, the other spatial.

1. *before/after*   *ten days before/after Christmas* . . . .
   ten miles before/after the turn-off . . . .

2. *ahead of/behind*   . . . .
   . . . .

3. *from/to*   . . . .
   . . . .

4. *beginning of/end of*   . . . .
   . . . .

5. *for*   . . . .
   . . . .

6. *until (till)*   . . . .
   . . . .

7. *on*   . . . .
   . . . .

8. *in*   . . . .
   . . . .

9. *beyond*   . . . .
   . . . .

ASSIGNMENT
141**

Temporal and Spatial Reference: L1

One of the more interesting predictions for child language acquisition was conceived more than a couple of decades ago by H. Clark (1973: 54–5) as the **Complexity Hypothesis**:

> Given two terms A and B, where B requires all the rules of application of A plus one more in addition, A will normally be acquired before B.

Clark illustrates application of the principle with the prepositions *in*, *into*, and *out of*:

Preposition	Rules of application
A *in* B	(1) B denotes a three-dimensional enclosed space
A *into* B	(1) B denotes a three-dimensional enclosed space (2) A is moving in one direction (3) The direction is positive
A *out of* B	(1) B denotes a three-dimensional enclosed space (2) A is moving in one direction (3) The direction is positive (4) Rule (3) is not the case

(continued)

1. What then does the Complexity Hypothesis predict regarding order of acquisition for the following pairs:

far/near	*to/from*	*above/below*
long/short	*into/out of*	*on top of/underneath*
high/low	*onto/off*	*up/down*
tall/short		*over/under*
deep/shallow		*ahead/behind*
wide/narrow		*in front of/in back of*
thick/thin		*before/after*

2. What does the Complexity Hypothesis predict regarding those pairs that serve as both spatial and temporal referents? That is, which kind of reference would be acquired first and why?

3. Finally, do the following documented child L1 examples have a bearing on the answer to the previous question?

    Friday is covering Saturday and Sunday so I can't have Saturday and Sunday if I don't go through Friday

    Can I have any reading behind the dinner?

ASSIGNMENT 142** Deixis with *come* and *go* (I)

Discussion of the use of the verbs *come* and *go* commonly refers to notions like **motion toward the speaker** for *come*, **motion away from the speaker** for *go*, and so on, as seen in Assignment 139. In truth, however, analysis of deixis with *come* and *go* is much more intricate than this. Consider the following sets of examples, where each set (A)–(D) introduces an element of additional complexity. All the complexity concerns essentially three concepts: (1) **motion toward/away from**, (2) **location of speaker/addressee**, and (3) **coding time vs. reference time**. Additionally involved in the data in (D) is the notion of location of **home base**.

(A) (1)   *Please come in*
      (2)   *Please go away*

(B) (3)   *He came here before I left*
      (4)   *He went there after I left*

(C) (5)   *I'll come there now/soon*
      (6)   *We* [inclusive or exclusive] *will go there now/soon*
      (7)   *We* [exclusive] *will come there now/soon*
      (8)   *Let's go/*come there now/soon*

(D) (9)   *I came over to your place, but you weren't home*
      10)   *I went over to Bob's place, but he wasn't home*
     (11) **I came over to Bob's place, but he wasn't home*

(continued)

State a generalization compatible with each successive set of data and in terms of the above three concepts:

(A) motion: *toward or away from* . . . .

location: *of speaker* . . . .

time: . . . .

(B) motion: . . . .

location: . . . .

time: . . . .

(C) motion: . . . .

location: . . . .

time: . . . .

(D) motion: . . . .

location: . . . .

time: . . . .

Collapse the above generalizations into two single statements – one each for *come* and *go* – in terms of whether the speaker is or is not at the goal of motion at coding and/or reference time.

come:

go:

_____
ASSIGNMENT # Deixis with *bring*
143**   # and *take*: L1

Look once more at the conditions for the use of the deictic verbs *come* and *go* as demonstrated in the previous exercise:

come: The speaker IS at the goal of motion at either coding time or reference time.

go: The speaker IS NOT at the goal of motion at coding time.

Directly related in a causal sense to *come* and *go* are the deictic verbs *bring* and *take* – i.e. *bring* = "cause to come" and *talk* = "cause to go." Moreover, *come* and *bring* bear an analogous relation to *go* and *take* in terms of their conditions of use. That is, just as *come* is **positively** specified for speaker location, so is *bring*; just as *go* is **negatively** specified for speaker location, so is *take*.
 Consider now the following observations on the L1 acquisition of *bring* and *take* by children ranging in age from 4 to 7:

(age 3   *come* produced before *go*)

age 4   *bring* first produced as a functioning term (*come* and *go* generally used correctly)

age 5   *take* first produced and as a synonym for *bring*

age 6   *bring* used correctly in *bring* situations; *bring* and *take* used randomly in *take* situations

age 7   *bring* and *take* used correctly

Although the acquisition order for the four deictic verbs at issue is thus fairly transparent, the more interesting question is why the ordering should be as it appears to be.

(continued)

Recall from Assignment 141 the **Complexity Hypothesis**, repeated here for convenience:

> Given two terms A and B, where B requires all the rules of application of A plus one more in addition, A will normally be acquired before B.

Taking the Complexity Hypothesis together with the conditions for the use of the deictics *come* and *go*, as stated above, provide a very brief accounting (at least in terms of the production findings tabulated) of the order of acquisition of all four deictic verbs, *come/go/bring/take*:

ASSIGNMENT
144*

Deixis with *come* and *go* (II)

In addition to their deictic characteristics already observed (Assignment 142), *come* and *go* enter into extended idiomatic usage in a systematic way, as described by E. Clark (1974). Write a form of *come/came* or *go/went*, whichever sounds right, in the blanks below. Then try to state a generalization that accounts for the choice.

1. *He* .... *into a frenzy.*
2. *She* .... *round to our point of view.*
3. *He* .... *out of his mind.*
4. *She* .... *into a lot of money.*
5. *He* .... *into a coma.*
6. *They* .... *to an understanding.*
7. *The motor* .... *dead.*
8. *The motor* .... *back to life.*
9. *They* .... *to realize their mistakes.*
10. *The meat* .... *bad.*
11. *Her dreams* .... *true.*
12. *She* .... *blind/deaf.*
13. *An idea* .... *to me.*
14. *The milk* .... *sour.*
15. *He* .... *bald.*
16. *He didn't* .... *up to our expectations.*
17. *The animals* .... *astray.*
18. *Which team* .... *in first?*
19. *He's about to* .... *bankrupt.*

(continued)

20. She .... back to her senses.

21. He .... of age.

22. She .... up with the best solution.

23. The bread .... stale.

24. She .... bananas.

25. They .... into receivership.

26. They .... off the deep end.

27. They .... through with flying colors.

28. All his plans .... awry.

29. You can't .... wrong.

30. His temperature .... up. [It WAS 96]

31. His temperature .... up. [It WAS 98.6]

32. The temperature .... down yesterday. [It WAS 106]

33. The temperature .... down yesterday. [It WAS 70]

34. The Republicans .... into office in 1980.

35. The Republicans .... out of office in 1992.

36. Bill Clinton .... through a lot.

37. John Major over......... /under.......... a lot.

38. The plane .... down near the lake.

Generalization:

Iconicity: L1
145*

In his study of iconicity, Haiman (1985: 1) writes that "linguistic forms are frequently the way they are because, like diagrams, they resemble the conceptual structures they are used to convey." A variant of this claim has been expressed by Slobin (1985: 228) for child language acquisition as "what belongs together mentally is placed close together syntactically."

Consider the example below quoted from the Slobin paper (1985: 225):

> There is a subset of mental verbs with optional *not*-transportation (*think, want, anticipate, expect, believe*). Children treat *think* as an ordinary complement-taking verb, maintaining negation in the embedded sentence (e.g. *I think it's not fulled up to the top*), although parental speech generally has the negative in the embedding sentence (e.g. *I don't think the man wants to taste it*).

Briefly, which person (child or adult) is observing **iconicity**, and in what way?

ASSIGNMENT 146* Iconicity and Temporal Adjunct Clauses: L1

Figuring in Assignments 132–4 was the **given–new principle,** or the general tendency to let that which is already known to the hearer or reader – i.e. **given** information – occur early in the sentence and that which is newly raised to consciousness – i.e. **new** information – occur later in the sentence. **Given** and **new**, it was noted, bear rough correspondence to the Prague School concepts of **theme** and **rheme**.

A number of L1 acquisition researchers, as reported by Karmiloff-Smith (1992: 461), have noted that young children often have difficulty in understanding sentences in which the temporal order of events is other than the order in which those events are mentioned in the sentence – a contravention of **iconicity**. An example of such a sentence would be (a), where the event of "going upstairs" occurred AFTER that of "washing":

(a) *Before the boy went upstairs, the girl washed the boy.*

On the other hand, children have much less difficulty understanding – and in fact actually PRODUCE – longer sentences in which iconicity is still contravened but redundancy has been added, as in (b):

(b) *The boy went upstairs, and before the boy went upstairs, the girl washed the boy.*

Taking into consideration both **iconicity** and the **given–new principle,** how (briefly) would you want to account for the child's preference for sentences like (b) over those like (a)?

ASSIGNMENT 147** Iconicity and Temporal Adjunct Clauses: L2

The following, statements are to be found in Tai (1985): "Chinese grammar refers to principles corresponding to the conceptual world more than grammatical rules operating on syntactic and morphological categories" (p. 63). "Slobin (1966) has shown that sentence comprehension is complicated when the order of elements in surface structure deviates from the perceptual order" (p. 64).

Goodluck and Birch (1988) did a study of the acquisition of some late-learned L2 English rules, including subject control in adjunct clauses, by L1 speakers of Spanish and of Chinese. They ran an experiment in which the following questions (among others) were asked of their subjects:

Bob met John after selling the ticket to George
Who sold the ticket to George?

Hank interviewed Jim after writing a letter to Greg
Who wrote a letter to Greg?

Frank called up Joe after giving the TV to Bob
Who gave the TV to Bob?

For the learners with lower proficiency (the experimenters' "level 1"), it is noteworthy that responses indicating that *who* is interpreted (correctly) as questioning the **subject** of the main clause were given by 67 percent of the Spanish-speaking learners but by only 33 percent of the Chinese speakers. The authors note that in Chinese temporal clauses are allowed only sentence-initially and conclude that "the greater error rate with this construction ... may be attributable ... to difficulty in dealing with a structural configuation that is unfamiliar" (1988: 111).

With respect to the above observations of Tai and of Slobin, what else might be taken into consideration in analyzing the results of the Goodluck and Birch experiment?

ASSIGNMENT 148* Iconicity and Progressive Aspect: L2

The relationship of language to thought has long been of interest to language researchers. One of the more important hypotheses bearing on this relationship has been termed the **complexity principle**:

COMPLEXITY IN THOUGHT TENDS TO BE REFLECTED IN COMPLEXITY OF EXPRESSION.

In the words of H. Clark and Clark (1977: 523), "broadly speaking, the more complex the expression, the more complex the thought it reflects." It has been noted by Kellerman (1983: 127) that inappropriate overuse of L2 English progressive aspect by advanced L1 Dutch learners may be an example of the complexity principle at work in SLA. The relevant data, taken from written production, are the following, where bracketed material represents the context of the sentence in question (in *italics*):

(a)   [Last year he took his exam]
      Day after day he was swotting for it

(b)   [I tried to find shelter somewhere]
      It was raining for hours

(c)   [What did you do yesterday?]
      Between 3 and 4 I was skating, and between 4 and 5 I was reading a book

Briefly, in what way could one claim that examples like these have been shaped by the complexity principle?

$\overline{\text{SECTION C}}$ **Word Formation**

ASSIGNMENT 149* Bound Morphology: L1

A number of different factors seem to play a role in determining the order in which various morphemes are acquired by children learning their native language. Consider just the *-ed* past tense morpheme and the *-s* 3rd person singular present tense morpheme in English. With reference to each of the 'determining factors' in L1 acquisition listed below, predict the order in which *-ed* and *-s* are likely to be acquired and check the corresponding column. (Note: some factors predict *-ed* before *-s*, some *-s* before *-ed*.) If no ordering is predicted, check both columns.

	-ed → *-s*	*-s* → *-ed*
1. one-to-one relationship between form and meaning	✓	. . .
2. allomorphic variation	. . .	. . .
3. capacity for being stressed	. . .	. . .
4. discernible semantic function	. . .	. . .
5. lack of exceptions	. . .	. . .
6. syllabicness	. . .	. . .
7. obligatoriness	. . .	. . .
8. absence of homophones	. . .	. . .
9. occurrence in word-final position	. . .	. . .

ASSIGNMENT 150* Bound and Free Morphology: L1/L2 (I)

A considerable amount of language acquisition research of the 1970s is repres-ented by the so-called "morpheme studies," or the documentation of the emer-gence in L1 and L2 English of a small class of morphemes, both bound and free. These morphemes are the following:

PLU(ral -S): the plural inflection on nouns (*hats*)

POSS(essive -S): the possessive inflectional affix (*Ed's* hat)

3rdP(erson -S): the agreement suffix on present-tense main verbs with 3rd-person subjects (*She wants help*)

ART(icle): the definite and indefinite article forms (*the, a*)

AUX: the conjugated forms of the auxiliary *be* appearing with verbs in the progressive (*She is/'s sleeping*)

REG(ular) PAST: the regular past-tense suffix (*She wanted help*)

IRREG(ular) PAST: past-tense inflection marked by other than -*ed* (She *slept*)

COP(ula): the conjugated forms of the copula *be* (*am, is*, etc.)

V-ing: the present participle suffix (*She's sleeping*)

Identify these morphemes as either **bound (B)** or **free (F)**:

1. PLU   . . .
2. POSS   . . .
3. 3rdP   . . .
4. ART   . . .
5. AUX   . . .

6. REG PAST   . . .
7. IRREG PAST   . . .
8. COP   . . .
9. V-ing   . . .

Name: _____   Date: __ / __ / __   Class: _____

ASSIGNMENT **Bound and Free**
151* **Morphology: L1/L2 (II)**

The nine morphemes figuring in language acquisition research of the 1970s and identified in the previous assignment are arranged below roughly in the L1/L2 **orders of acquisition** tabulated in research of the period:

	L1	L2
earlier acquisition:	V-*ing* PLU IRREG PAST	V-*ing* COP AUX ART
	ART POSS COP	PLU IRREG PAST
later acquisition:	REG PAST 3rdP AUX	REG PAST 3rdP POSS

From a glance at this tabulation, it is clear that there are certain differences as well as similarities in the L1 and L2 orders. It is the differences that we will consider here. Beyond obvious contrasts in the acquisition times for individual morphemes – e.g. AUX is earlier in L2, later in L1 – what else might be discerned from these orders? Specifically:

(continued)

1. What can be said about TIMING in the acquisition of the above **bound** vs. **free** morphemes for L1 and L2?

2. What can be said about DISTRIBUTION in the acquisition of the above **free** morphemes for L1 and L2?

ASSIGNMENT 152** Bound and Free Morphology: L1/L2 (III)

Modern linguistics has long recognized a general informal distinction between so-called **content words** and **function words**. The former are typically open-class items (new words can be created) with semantic structure – i.e. the major **lexical categories**: nouns, verbs, adjectives. The latter are typically closed-class items (no new words can be created) difficult to define in a dictionary sense – i.e. **non-lexical categories**: articles, deictics, auxiliaries, relative pronouns, complementizers, the preposition *of*, etc.

Recent linguistic research has begun to accord greater importance to these function words, leading to the need to extend the class of phrasal categories from the major lexicon (i.e. V, N, A, P) to function words. Accordingly, and as seen in the assignments of Part I, I(nflection), embracing (in simplified fashion) auxiliaries, modals, tense and agreement features, etc., projects to IP; C(omplementizer), represented by *that, for, if,* and possibly *whether,* projects to CP; and D(eterminer), embracing the articles, deictics, possessives, etc., projects to DP. As has already been noted, IP, CP, and DP, each now with its own internal structure, are phrasal projections of (appropriately termed) **functional categories,** to distinguish them from the lexical categories.

Reproduced below is the L1/L2 acquisition picture outlined in the previous assignment. For each morpheme class that instantiates a functional category of the kind just described, write next to it the phrasal projection of that category – namely, IP, CP, or DP. Assume that IRREG PAST and V-*ing* are **lexical** categories.

(continued)

	L1	L2

	L1	L2
earlier acquisition:	V-*ing*	V-*ing* ....
	PLU	COP ....
	IRREG PAST	AUX ....
		ART ....
	ART	PLU ....
	POSS	IRREG PAST ....
	COP	
	REG PAST	REG PAST ....
later acquisition:	3rdP	3rdP ....
	AUX	POSS ....

Based on the pattern of IP/DP entries now displayed above, what further observations can be made? Specifically, for which learning situation, L1 or L2:

1. do functional category projections seem to be available in the earlier stages?

2. does there seem to be a SEQUENCE in the emergence of IP/DP and what is it?

3. does there seem to be a sequence in the emergence of the sub-parts of IP vis-à-vis the morphological exponents of **agreement**?

4. do functional projections seem to emerge in reference to SPECIFIC categories rather than ACROSS categories?

5. is there a distinct division between the emergence of **lexical heads** and that of **inflectional heads**?

ASSIGNMENT 153* Bound Morphology: -*ed*

English abounds in constructions bearing structural surface similarity but under-lying fundamental differences, and ample demonstration of that can be found throughout these materials. Good examples would be the various kinds of verb phrase with a surface structure of V NP PP (Assignment 24), the seemingly similar clausal complement structures for *believe, want,* and *persuade* (Assign-ment 21), the identical-looking derived structures with raising verbs and control verbs (Assignment 45), the surface similarities of relative clause, noun comple-ment, and cleft sentence (Assignment 52), and so on. Surface deception of this kind is also to be seen in noun modification involving bound morphology. Consider the following examples:

(a)   *bored student*
(b)   *gifted child*
(c)   *shared information*
(d)   *melted ice cream*
(e)   *vanished civilization*

- The modifier in (a) is an adjective formed from the past participle of a so-called **psych-verb** (e.g. *excited, fascinated, discouraged,* etc.).

- The modifier in (b) is an adjective formed from a noun plus the **possessive** -*ed* suffix (e.g. *flowered, starred, louvered,* "*booted* and *spurred*," etc.).

- The modifier in (c) is formed from the past participle of a **transitive verb** (e.g. *discarded, invaded, modified, attempted,* etc.).

- The modifier in (d) is formed from the past participle of an **ergative verb** – cf. Assignment 71 – (e.g. *cooked, cracked, thawed, burned,* etc.).

- The modifier in (e) is formed from the past participle of an **unaccusative verb** – cf. Assignment 67 – (e.g. *perished, extended, spilled, transpired,* etc.)

Note that verbs in (a), (c), (d), and (e) are not limited to those whose past participles show **regular** -*ed* suffixation, since we also have *smitten lover* (a), **kept** *promise* (c), **torn** *curtain* (d), *the risen Christ* (e), etc.

(continued)

    Identify each of the examples below as one or another of the five types of two-word modification-plus-noun presented above. Use the following code:

PV for modification formed from a **psych-verb**

POSS for modification formed from **possessive** *-ed*

TV for modification formed from a **transitive verb**

EV for modification formed from an **ergative verb**

UV for modification formed from an **unaccusative verb**

1. .... *finished product*		13. .... *flawed plan*
2. .... *wrinkled paper*		14. .... *boiled egg*
3. .... *satisfied customer*		15. .... *fallen idol*
4. .... *gifted child*		16. .... *hidden agenda*
5. .... *failed solutions*		17. .... *tired workers*
6. .... *shelved books*		18. .... *broken window*
7. .... *forked tongue*		19. .... *broken promise*
8. .... *botched operation*		20. .... *talented artist*
9. .... *interested parties*		21. .... *sunken ship*
10. .... *grown men*		22. .... *decomposed body*
11. .... *hardened criminal*		23. .... *spoken language*
12. .... *hardened substance*		24. .... *startled animal*

ASSIGNMENT **Compounds**
154*

Compounding in English embraces a variety of possible internal structure – for example, *movie star* (N + N), *nationwide* (N + A), *undervalue* (P + V). Furthermore, the entire compound itself functions as a grammatical category – e.g. N (*movie star*), A (*nationwide*), V (*undervalue*), etc. Nouns are by far the category appearing most frequently in compounds. Other features of compounding are the following:

- Regular number inflection for a left-most noun is almost always limited to the singular:
  (cage for birds) = *bird cage* / cf. **birds cage*

- Some irregular plural nouns may remain intact:
  (marks made by teeth) = *teethmarks* / *toothmarks*
  (brush for teeth) = *toothbrush* / cf. **teethbrush*

- **Pluralia tantum** (i.e. nouns normally occurring only in the plural) remain intact:
  (dryer of clothes) = *clothes dryer* / cf. **clothe dryer*

- The standard stress pattern for two-member compounds in English is primary–tertiary:
  bláckbòard   bítterswèet   óverdòse   píckpòcket

  with a few occurring as secondary–primary:
  jêt bláck

   For each of the compounds listed below, indicate its internal **structure** as well as its grammatical **category**. Among the left-most members, identify as well any **irregular plurals** and **pluralia tantum**. Mark the stress pattern (´ ` or ^ ´) over each compound:

(continued)

	COMPOUND	STRUCTURE	CATEGORY	IRREG PLURAL	PLURALIA TANTUM
1.	*péople móver*	*N + N*	*noun*	....	*people*
2.	*bitter-sweet*	... + ...	....	....	....
3.	*onlooker*	... + ...	....	....	....
4.	*pickpocket*	... + ...	....	....	....
5.	*turntable*	... + ...	....	....	....
6.	*dry clean*	... + ...	....	....	....
7.	*dues payment*	... + ...	....	....	....
8.	*mice-infested*	... + ...	....	....	....
9.	*widespread*	... + ...	....	....	....
10.	*day dream*	... + ...	....	....	....
11.	*age old*	... + ...	....	....	....
12.	*pants leg*	... + ...	....	....	....
13.	*cry baby*	... + ...	....	....	....
14.	*bathroom*	... + ...	....	....	....
15.	*accident-prone*	... + ...	....	....	....
16.	*earnings ratio*	... + ...	....	....	....
17.	*handyman*	... + ...	....	....	....
18.	*teeth cleaning*	... + ...	....	....	....
19.	*eye examination*	... + ...	....	....	....
20.	*car sick*	... + ...	....	....	....
21.	*thieves market*	... + ...	....	....	....
22.	*Anglo-French*	... + ...	....	....	....
23.	*deer crossing*	... + ...	....	....	....
24.	*thanksgiving*	... + ...	....	....	....
25.	*war weary*	... + ...	....	....	....
26.	*oxen-handler*	... + ...	....	....	....
27.	*cow puncher*	... + ...	....	....	....
28.	*rock hard*	... + ...	....	....	....
29.	*scarecrow*	... + ...	....	....	....
30.	*sun bathe*	... + ...	....	....	....

(continued)

Name: _____   Date: __ / __ / __   Class: _____

In which examples do the stress patterns appear to be exceptions to the more general primary–tertiary pattern for compounds?

What simple generalization can you make in comparing the grammatical **structure** of the compound and the grammatical **category** of the compound? Think in terms of which member of the compound has to be the **head**.

ASSIGNMENT 155* Prefixation (*un-*)

Introduced in Assignment 18 was the [± V/N] feature specification for the four major lexical categories: N, V, A, P. Noted there was the fact that a SINGLE feature such as [+V] would therefore constitute the natural class comprising verbs and adjectives. Additional support for the feature analysis can be seen in the area of derivational morphology. It has been observed, for example, that only adjectives and verbs permit direct *un-* **prefixation**, not nouns or prepositions:

> *unafraid, unaware, unfit, unkind* [**Adjectives**]
> *undo, untie, unfold, unpack, unravel* [**Verbs**]
> **unfear, *unconvention, *unjoy* [**Nouns**]
> *uninside, *unby, *unon, *unfrom* [**Prepositions**]

1. Which of the following words could be considered counter-examples to this claim? Why are the others NOT counter-examples?

    unbeliever

    undoing

    unlikelihood

    unrest

    unsuitability

    untruth

    unsophistication

    unconsciousness

    unreceptivity

2. Is there anything unusual for you about the following:
    unhorse, unearth, unchurch

ASSIGNMENT 156*   Prefixation (*un-* + Verb): L1

The prefix *un-* occurs with many verbs: e.g. *uncover, uncoil, undress, unfasten, unfold, unlock, unroll, untangle, untie, unwind,* etc. Yet there are restrictions on such prefixation, since we cannot say, for example, **unbreak, *undry, *unhang, *unheat, *unlift, *unmelt, *unopen, *unpress, *unspill,* etc., all of these examples cited by Whorf (1956). Young children, however, do coin inadmissible words like these very early in their learning experience, as in the following examples recorded by Bowerman (1982):

(a) *I hate you! And I'll never **unhate** you or nothing*!

(b) *I'm gonna **unhang** it* [taking stocking down from fireplace]

(c) *How do you make it **unsprinkle**?* [after getting faucet to sprinkle]

(d) *. . . and then **unpress** it out* [showing how to get playdough out of a mold]

(e) *He tippitoed to the graveyard and **unburied** her* [telling ghost story]

(f) *Will you **unopen** this?* [wants daddy to take lid off styrofoam cooler]

1. Can you identify a set of semantic characteristics that loosely define the POSSIBLE *un-*verb formations like those illustrated?

(continued)

2. Judging from examples (a)–(f) and notwithstanding their deviance from adult speech, what aspect of the meaning of *un-* have children actually succeeded in learning?

3. Is there anything particularly unusual about the use of *unopen* in (f)?

ASSIGNMENT # **Prefixation**
157* (*un-* and *in-*)

Enter the appropriate written **negative prefix,** i.e. (variants of) *in-/un-*, for each of the words listed below, then answer the questions that follow. (It is also possible that in some dialects an occasional word can occur with both prefixes, perhaps with different meanings.)

1.	*un,able*	*in ability*	21.	*clear*	
2.	*equality*	*equal*	22.	*true*	
3.	*legal*	*lawful*	23.	*personal*	
4.	*thinkable*	*conceivable*	24.	*grammatical*	
5.	*readable*	*legible*	25.	*polite*	
6.	*literate*	*lettered*	26.	**munize*	
7.	*justice*	*just*	27.	*interesting*	
8.	*attended*	*attention*	28.	*popular*	
9.	*edible*	*eatable*	29.	*famous*	
10.	*dependent*	*dependable*	30.	*possible*	
11.	*balance*	*balanced*	31.	*convenient*	
12.	**reparable*	*repairable*	32.	*forgiving*	
13.	*regulated*	*regular*	33.	*practical*	
14.	*credible*	*believable*	34.	*potent*	
15.	**dubitably*	*doubtedly*	35.	*important*	
16.	*rational*	*reasonable*	36.	*definite*	
17.	*ceasing*	**cessant*	37.	*certain*	
18.	**evitable*	*avoidable*	38.	*formal*	
19.	*explicable*	*explainable*	39.	*natural*	
20.	*faithful*	**fidel*	40.	*usual*	

(continued)

41. . . . . .*perfect*   45. . . . . .*capable*

42. . . . . .*finite*   46. . . . . .*moral*

43. . . . . .*necessary*   47. . . . . .*kind*

44. . . . . .*familiar*   48. . . . . .*likely*

(a) Which of the two prefixes shows **allomorphic variation**?   . . . . .
     What are the **allomorphs** for this prefix?

     . . . .

(b) Which of the two prefixes sometimes attracts the **shift of
     primary stress?**   . . . . .
     Cite the examples in which **stress shift** occurs:

     . . . .

     . . . .

(c) For which of the two prefixations is the stem sometimes a
     non-occurring word in the language?   . . . . .
     Cite the examples of **non-occurring words:**

     . . . .

     . . . .

(d) Which of the two prefixes is the more **productive** one?   . . . . .

ASSIGNMENT 158* Derivational Suffixation

Assignment B at the beginning of this book drew attention to the commonly recognized distinction between **inflectional** and **derivational** suffixes. It was noted that derivational suffixes – e.g. *-ment, -ness, -ize, -er*, etc. – show the following characteristics:

- alteration of the grammatical category of the stem:

  compute + *er* = computer   (cf. *computer* + *s* = *computers*)
    [V]   [N]   [N]   [N]

- location closer to the stem:

  compute + *er* + *s*   (cf. **compute* + *s* + *er*)

- more than one permitted:

  compute + *er* + *ize* + *ation*   (cf. **comput* + *ed* + *ing*)

- more limited productivity:

  argument, **decidement*,   (cf. *arguments*, *decisions*,
  *coverment, **refusement*)   *coverages*, *refusals*)

In truth, however, a distinction can be drawn among derivational suffixes themselves in terms of properties such as the following:

		(1) (yes)	(2) (no)
■ deformation of stem:	(*example*)	exempl-*ify*	
	(*random*)		random-*ize*
■ stress shift:	(*húman*)	humán-*ity*	húman-*ness*
■ vowel change:	(*nation*)	nation-*al*	nation-*hood*
	/e/	/æ/	/e/
■ low productivity:	(*correct*)	correct-*ion*	correct-*ness*
	(*flexible*)	flexibil-*ity*	flexible-*ness*
	(*accurate*)	accurac-*y*	accurate-*ness*

Words bearing derivational suffixes thus fall into two groups (1) and (2) by the above criteria, and these two will figure prominently in the next assignment.

(continued)

Each of the following words contains one or more derivational suffixes. With reference to the set of properties outlined above, indicate by writing "1" or "2" which of the two types the suffix in **bold type** represents. In making some of these identifications, it may help to compare additional words bearing the same suffix:

1. ..... *chris**tian***		15. ..... *prefer**ence***
2. ..... *god**ly***		16. ..... *prefer**ential***
3. ..... *friend**ship***		17. ..... *stand**ing***
4. ..... *chocol**aty***		18. ..... *tal**ented***
5. ..... *tele**graphy***		19. ..... *produc**tive***
6. ..... *work**er***		20. ..... *standoff**ish***
7. ..... *cod**ify***		21. ..... *apolo**getic***
8. ..... *system**atize***		22. ..... *coer**cion***
9. ..... *clue**less***		23. ..... *Trotsky**ite***
10. ..... *aristo**cracy***		24. ..... *Stalin**ist***
11. ..... *streng**then***		25. ..... *friendli**ness***
12. ..... *liveli**hood***		26. ..... *insan**ity***
13. ..... *explan**ation***		27. ..... *flavor**ful***
14. ..... *republican**ism***		28. ..... *arri**val***

ASSIGNMENT 159** Level Ordering

In the previous two assignments, a sharp distinction was drawn between two pre-fixes and between sets of suffixes, both based on occurrence or non-occurrence of such features as **allomorphic variation, location vis-à-vis the stem, attraction of primary stress, co-occurrence possibility, stem deformation, vowel change, category change,** and **productivity.** Subsets of these criteria actually serve to distinguish the entire range of derivational and inflectional morphology in Eng-lish. We have already seen that when there is a combination of suffixes from different subsets – namely, derivational and inflectional – the former always precedes the latter (e.g. *codified* [*code* + *ify* + *ed*], not **codedify*). The effects of mixing extends, however, even WITHIN the derivational suffixation encountered in the previous assignment – i.e. the subtypes (a) and (b) – where type (a) will precede type (b). For example:

(George Bernard) *Shaw + ian* $\longrightarrow$ *shavian + ism* $\longrightarrow$ *shavianism*
          (1)   (1)   (2)   (1) (2)

not: *Shaw + ism* $\longrightarrow$ **shavism + ian* $\longrightarrow$ **shavismian*
        (2)   (2)   (1)   (2) (1)

Facts like these have led to the establishment of **levels** of derivation, where the word-formation rules of an earlier level are necessarily invoked before those of a later one, a procedure termed **level ordering.** Entering into the picture as well are the facts of noun plurals within compounds encountered in Assignment 154 – i.e. *people mover* vs. *piano mover* (**pianos mover*). The number of levels in the formation of words in English has been put at four. Ranging over the four levels would be **regular inflections, irregular inflections,** the two types of **derivational suffixation** (cf. the previous assignment), the two types of **prefixation** (Assignment 155), **compounding,** and **pluralia tantum** (Assignment 154).

(continued)

1. Drawing upon the examples encountered so far in the assignments of this section, enter into the hierarchy below those of the word-formation phenomena that apply at each of the four levels:

   Level One:

   . . . .

   Level Two:

   . . . .

   Level Three:

   . . . .

   Level Four:

   . . . .

2. It has been noted that not all the vast numbers of words with morphological structure are consistent with the level-ordering hypothesis. Two of these, actually quite common words, are listed below. Briefly, in what way would they be analyzed as counter-examples?

   civilization

   . . . .

   ungrammaticality (cf. Assignment 155)

   . . . .

   . . . .

   . . . .

   . . . .

3. The two words listed below also violate level ordering and are judged UNgrammatical. Again briefly, in what way do they constitute a violation?

   dinner-theatrical (*dinner-theatre* + *ical*)

   . . . .

   powerlessity

   . . . .

   . . . .

ASSIGNMENT
160**
Level Ordering: L1

A number of researchers have been interested in the status of level ordering with respect to language learning in childhood. A rough summary of the research findings to date that are relevant to level ordering might include the following:

- Regular plurals are rarely found as left member of a two-word compound; it is the singular form that occurs.

- Irregular plurals occur as left member of a two-word compound, and with greater frequency than in adult speech.

- Unreduced pluralia tantum often occur as left member of a two-word compound.

- Innovative denominal verbs abound (e.g. *I broomed her, How was it shoelaced?, You axed the wood*).

- Innovative deverbal nouns are rarely found.

- Innovative prefixation with *un-* abounds; innovative *in-* prefixation is not found (cf. Assignment 157).

- Children give more regular plural responses for exocentric nouns than for endocentric nouns.

(continued)

   With reference to the above, consider the matter of what the child is likely or unlikely to hear in the adult input. What conclusions about **level ordering in child-language acquisition** can plausibly be drawn from these observations?

Bibliography

Akmajian, A., R. Demers, and R. Harnish (eds). 1990. *Linguistics: An Introduction to Language and Communication*. Cambridge, MA: MIT Press.

Allen, J. 1993. Markedness and ordering in L1 and L2 grammars. Unpublished paper, USC.

Altman, R. 1984. Assessing modal proficiency in English as a second language. Unpublished PhD dissertation, University of Southern California.

Andersen, R. 1984. The one to one principle of interlanguage construction. *Language Learning* 34: 77–95.

Andersen, R. 1991. Developmental sequences: the emergence of aspect marking in second language acquisition. In Huebner and Ferguson (1991).

Andersen, R., and Y. Shirai. 1994. Discourse motivation for some cognitive acquisition principles. *Studies in Second Language Acquisition* 16: 133–56.

Aoun, J. 1985. *A Grammar of Anaphora*. Cambridge, MA: MIT Press.

Archibald, J. 1994. A formal model of learning L2 prosodic phonology. *Second Language Research* 10: 215–45.

Atkinson, M. 1992. *Children's Syntax: An Introduction to Principles and Parameters Theory*. Oxford: Blackwell.

Bardovi-Harlig, K. 1994. Anecdote or evidence? Evaluating support for hypotheses concerning the development of tense and aspect. In E. Tarone, S. Gass, and A. Cohen (eds), *Research Methodology in Second Language Acquisition*. Hillsdale, NJ: Lawrence Erlbaum.

Beilin, H. 1975. *Studies in the Cognitive Basis of Language Development*. New York: Academic Press.

Bellugi, U. 1967. The acquisition of negation. Unpublished doctoral dissertation, Harvard.

Bialystok, E. 1983. On learning language form and language function. *Interlanguage Studies Bulletin* 7: 54–70.

Bickerton, D. 1981. *Roots of Language*. Ann Arbor: Karoma Publishers.

Bley-Vroman, R., S. Felix, and G. Ioup. 1988. The accessibility of Universal Grammar in adult language learning. *Second Language Research* 4: 1–32.

Bloom, L. 1970. *Language Development: Form and Function in Emerging Grammars*. Cambridge, MA: MIT Press.

Bloom, P. 1993. Grammatical continuity in language development: the case of subjectless sentences. *Linguistic Inquiry* 24: 721–34.

Bloom, P. (ed.). 1994. *Language Acquisition: Core Readings*. Cambridge. MA: MIT Press.

Bloom, P. 1995. Possible names: the role of syntax–semantics mappings in the acquisition of nominals. In Gleitman and Landau (1995).

Bowerman, M. 1982. Reorganizational processes in lexical and syntactic development. In Wanner and Gleitman (1982).

Bresnan, J. 1978. Contraction and the transformational cycle in English. Indiana University Linguistics Club.

Brown, R. 1973. *A First Language: The Early Stages*. Cambridge, MA: Harvard University Press.

Brown, R., and U. Bellugi. 1964. Three processes in the child's acquisition of syntax. *Harvard Educational Review* 34: 133–51.

Bybee, J. 1985. *Morphology*. Amsterdam: John Benjamins.

Cairns, H., D. McDaniel, J. Hsu, and M. Rapp. 1994. A longitudinal study of principles of control and pronominal reference in child English. *Language* 70: 260–88.

Carrell, P. 1978. The Given–New strategy: testing presupposition and assertion in L1 and L2. In C. Blatchford and J. Schachter (eds), *On TESOL '78*. Washington: Teachers of English to Speakers of Other Languages.

Chafe, W. 1976. Givenness, contrastiveness, definiteness, subjects, topics, and point of view. In C. Li (ed.), *Subject and Topic*. New York: Academic Press.

Chomsky, C. 1969. *The Acquisition of Syntax in Children from 5 to 10*. Cambridge, MA: MIT Press.

Chomsky, N. 1957. *Syntactic Structures*. The Hague: Mouton.

Chomsky, N. 1981. *Lectures on Government and Binding*. Dordrecht: Foris.

Chomsky, N. 1986. *Barriers*. Cambridge, MA: MIT Press.

Chomsky, N. 1995. *The Minimalist Program*. Cambridge, MA: MIT Press.

Clahsen, H. 1981. *Spracherwerb in der Kindheit*. Tübingen: Gunter Narr.

Clahsen, H. 1984. The acquisition of German word order: a test case for cognitive approaches to L2 development. In R. Andersen (ed.), *Second Language: A Crosslinguistic Perspective*. Rowley, MA: Newbury House.

Clark, E. 1974. Normal states and evaluative viewpoints. *Language* 50: 316–32.

Clark, E. 1982. The young word-maker: a case study of innovation in the child's lexicon. In Wanner and Gleitman (1982).

Clark, H. 1973. Space, time, semantics, and the child. In T. Moore (ed.), *Cognitive Development and the Acquisition of Language*. New York: Academic Press.

Clark, H., and E. Clark. 1977. *Psychology and Language*. New York: Harcourt Brace Jovanovich.

Clark, H., and S. Haviland. 1977. The Given–New Contract. In R. Freedle (ed.), *Discourse Production and Comprehension*, vol. 1. Norwood, NJ: Ablex.

Comrie, B. 1976. *Aspect*. Cambridge: Cambridge University Press.

Comrie, B. 1987. Why linguists need language acquirers. In Rutherford (1987a).

Comrie, B. 1989. *Language Universals and Linguistic Typology*. Chicago: University of Chicago Press.

Comrie, B. 1990. Second language acquisition and language universals research. *Studies in Second Language Acquisition* 12: 209–18.

Cook, V. 1993. *Linguistics and Second Language Acquisition*. New York: St Martin's Press.

Cook, V., and M. Newson. 1996. *Chomsky's Universal Grammar*. Second edition. Oxford: Blackwell.

Cowper, E. 1992. *A Concise Introduction to Syntactic Theory*. Chicago: Chicago University Press.

Crain, S. 1994. Language acquisition in the absence of experience. In P. Bloom (1994).

Dechert, H., and M. Raupach (eds). 1989. *Transfer in Language Production*. Norwood, NJ: Ablex.

Déprez, V., and A. Pierce. 1993. Negation and functional Projections in early grammar. *Linguistic Inquiry* 24: 25–67.

Déprez, V., and A. Pierce. 1994. Crosslinguistic evidence for functional projections in early child grammar. In Hoekstra and Schwartz (1994).

de Villiers, J., and T. Roeper. 1995. Barriers, binding, and acquisition of the DP–NP distinction. *Language Acquisition* 4: 73–104.

Eckman, F. 1977. Markedness and the contrastive analysis hypothesis. *Language Learning* 27: 315–30.

Eckman, F. (ed.). 1993. *Confluence: Linguistics, L2 Acquisition, Speech Pathology*. Amsterdam: John Benjamins.

Eckman, F., L. Bell, and D. Nelson (eds). 1984. *Universals of Second Language Acquisition*. Rowley, MA: Newbury House.

Eckman, F., L. Bell, and D. Nelson. 1988. On the generalization of relative clause construction in the acquisition of English as a second language. *Applied Linguistics* 9: 1–20.

Ellis, R. 1985. *Understanding Second Language Acquisition*. Oxford: Oxford University Press.

Emonds, J. 1976. *A Transformational Approach to English Syntax*. New York: Academic Press.

Eubank, L. (ed.). 1991a. *Point Counterpoint: Universal Grammar in the Second Language*. Amsterdam: John Benjamins.

Eubank, L. 1991b. Transfer or Universal Grammar: reply to Jordens. In Eubank (1991a).

Eubank, L., L. Selinker, and M. Sharwood Smith (eds). 1995. *The Current State of Interlanguage*. Amsterdam: John Benjamins.

Fillmore, C. 1971. *Santa Cruz Lectures on Deixis*. Bloomington, IN: Indiana University Linguistics Club.

Finer, D. 1991. Binding parameters in second language acquisition. In Eubank (1991a).

Fletcher, P., and M. Garman (eds). 1992. *Language Acquisition*. Second edition. Cambridge: Cambridge University Press.

Flynn, K. 1985. The acquisition of form and function: an analysis of the use of the perfect in the written discourse of adult second language learners. Unpublished PhD dissertation, University of Southern California.

Flynn, S., C. Foley, and D. Lardiere. 1991. The minimality principle in adult second language acquisition. Paper presented at the Second Language Research Forum, University of Southern California.

Foster, S. 1990. *The Communicative Competence of Young Children*. London: Longman.

Foster-Cohen, S. 1994. Exploring the boundary between syntax and pragmatics: relevance and the binding of pronouns. In Perera et al. (1994).

Frawley, W. 1992. *Linguistic Semantics*. Hillsdale, NJ: Lawrence Erlbaum.

Frazier, L., and J. de Villiers (eds). 1990. *Language Processing and Language Acquisition*. Dordrecht: Kluwer.

Gabrys, G., A. Weiner, and A. Lesgold. 1993. Learning by problem solving in a coached apprenticeship system. In M. Rabinowitz (ed.), *Cognitive Science Foundations of Instruction*. Hillsdale, NJ: Lawrence Erlbaum.

Gass, S., and J. Ard. 1987. Second language acquisition and the ontology of language universals. In Rutherford (1987a).

Gass, S., and J. Schachter (eds). 1989. *Linguistic Perspectives on Second Language Acquisition*. Cambridge: Cambridge University Press.

Gass, S., and L. Selinker. 1984. *Workbook in Second Language Acquisition*. Rowley, MA: Newbury House.

Gerken, L. 1991. The metrical basis for children's subjectless sentences. *Journal of Memory and Language* 30: 1–21.

Gibson, E., and K. Wexler. 1994. Triggers. *Linguistic Inquiry* 25: 407–54.

Givon, T. 1979. *On Understanding Grammar*. New York: Academic Press.

Givon, T. 1987. Universals of discourse structure and second language acquisition. In Rutherford (1987a).

Gleason, H. 1965. *Linguistics and English Grammar*. New York: Holt, Rinehart and Winston.

Gleitman, L., and B. Landau (eds). 1995. *The Acquisition of the Lexicon*. Cambridge, MA: MIT Press.

Goodluck, H. 1981. Children's grammar of complement–subject interpretation. In Tavakolian (1981).

Goodluck, H. 1991. *Language Acquisition: A Linguistic Introduction*. Oxford: Blackwell.

Goodluck, H., and D. Behne. 1992. Development in control and extraction. In Weissenborn et al. (1992).

Goodluck, H., and B. Birch. 1988. Late-learned rules in first and second language acquisition. In J. Pankhurst, M. Sharwood Smith, and P. Van Buren (eds), *Learnability and Second Languages: A Book of Readings*. Dordrecht: Foris.

Gordon, P. 1994. Level-ordering in lexical development. In P. Bloom (1994).

Green, G. 1980. Some wherefores of English inversions. *Language* 56: 582–601.

Greenberg, J. 1963. Some universals of grammar with particular reference to the order of meaningful elements. In J. Greenberg (ed.), *Universals of Language*. Cambridge, MA: MIT Press.

Grimshaw, J. 1990. *Argument Structure*. Cambridge, MA: MIT Press.

Gruber, J. 1967. Topicalization in child language. *Foundations of Language* 3: 37–65.

Grundy, P. 1995. *Doing Pragmatics*. London: Edward Arnold.

Guéron, J., and L. Haegeman. Forthcoming. *English Grammar: Syntax, Interpretation, and Variation*. Oxford: Blackwell.

Haegeman, L. 1994. *Introduction to Government and Binding Theory*. Second edition. Oxford: Blackwell.

Haiman, J. (ed.). 1985. *Iconicity in Syntax*. Amsterdam: John Benjamins.

Halmari, H. 1997. *Government and Codeswitching: Explaining American Finnish*. Amsterdam: John Benjamins.

Hamilton, R. 1994. Is implicational generalization unidirectional and maximal? Evidence from relativization instruction in a second language. *Language Learning* 44: 123–57.

Hammond, M. 1993. On the absence of category-changing prefixes in English. *Linguistic Inquiry* 24: 562–7.

Hartford, B. 1995. Zero anaphora in non-native texts: null object anaphora in Nepalese English. *Studies in Second Language Acquisition* 17: 245–61.

Hatch, E., and A. Lazaraton. 1991. *The Research Manual*. Rowley, MA: Newbury House.

Hawkins, J. 1977. The pragmatics of definiteness (parts I and II). *Linguistische Berichte* 47: 1–27 (part I), 48: 1–27 (part II).

Hawkins, J. 1987. Implicational universals as predictors of language acquisition. *Linguistics* 25: 453–73.

Hawkins, J. 1991. Language universals in relation to acquisition and change: a tribute to Roman Jakobson. In L. Waugh and S. Rudy (eds), *New Vistas in Grammar: Invariance and Variation*. Amsterdam: John Benjamins.

Hilles, S. 1991. Access to Universal Grammar in second language acquisition. In Eubank (1991a).

Hinds, J. 1983. Topic continuity in Japanese. In T. Givón (ed.), *Topic Continuity in Discourse: A Quantitative Cross-Linguistic Study*. Amsterdam: John Benjamins.

Hoekstra, T., and B. Schwartz (eds). 1994. *Language Acquisition Studies in Generative Grammar*. Amsterdam: John Benjamins.

Huang, C.-T.J. 1984. On the distribution and reference of empty pronouns. *Linguistic Inquiry* 15: 531–74.

Huddleston, R. 1984. *Introduction to the Grammar of English*. Cambridge: Cambridge University Press.

Huebner, T. 1979. Order of acquisition vs. dynamic paradigm: A comparison of method in interlanguage research. *TESOL Quarterly* 13: 21–8.

Huebner, T., and C. Ferguson (eds). 1991. *Crosscurrents in Second Language Acquisition and Linguistic Theories*. Amsterdam: John Benjamins.

Hyams, N. 1994. V2, null arguments and COMP projections. In Hoekstra and Schwartz (1994).

Hyams, N., and O. Jaeggli. 1989. The null subject parameter and parametric theory. In Jaeggli and Safir (1989).

Hyams, N., and K. Wexler. 1993. On the grammatical basis of null subjects in child language. *Linguistic Inquiry* 24: 421–59.

Ingram, D. 1989. *First Language Acquisition*. Cambridge: Cambridge University Press.

Jaeggli, O., and N. Hyams. 1988. Morphological uniformity and the setting of the null subject parameter. In J. Blevins and J. Carter (eds), *Proceedings of NELS 18*. Amherst, MA: University of Massachusetts.

Jaeggli, O., and K. Safir (eds). 1989. *The Null Subject Parameter*. Dordrecht: Kluwer.

Jain, M. 1974. Error analysis: source, cause and significance. In J. Richards (ed.), *Error Analysis: Perspectives on Second Language Acquisition*. London: Longman.

Johnson, J., and E. Newport. 1991. Critical period effects on universal properties of languages: the status of subjacency in the acquisition of a second language. *Cognition* 39: 215–58.

Jordens, P. 1991. Linguistic knowledge in second language acquisition. In Eubank (1991a).

Juffs, A., and M. Harrington. 1995. Parsing effects in second language sentence processing: subject and object asymmetries in wh-extraction. *Studies in Second Language Acquisition* 17: 483–516.

Karmiloff-Smith, A. 1992. Some fundamental aspects of language development after age 5. In Fletcher and Garman (1992).

Kayne, R. 1994. *The Antisymmetry of Syntax*. Cambridge, MA: MIT Press.

Keenan, E., and B. Comrie. 1977. Noun phrase accessibility and universal grammar. *Linguistic Inquiry* 8: 63–99.

Kellerman, E. 1983. Now you see it, now you don't. In S. Gass and L. Selinker (eds), *Language Transfer in Language Learning*. Rowley, MA: Newbury House.

Keyser, S., and T. Roeper. 1984. On the middle and ergative constructions in English. *Linguistic Inquiry* 15: 381–416.

Kim, J., G. Marcus, S. Pinker, M. Hollander, and M. Coppola. (1994). Sensitivity of children's inflection to grammatical structure. In Perera et al. (1994).

Kumpf, L. 1984. Temporal systems and universality in interlanguage. In Eckman et al. (1984).

Kuno, S. 1973. *The Structure of the Japanese Language*. Cambridge, MA: MIT Press.

Kuno, S. 1976. Subject, theme, and the speaker's empathy – a reexamination of relativization phenomena. In C. Li (ed.), *Subject and Topic*. New York: Academic Press.

Larsen-Freeman, D., and M. Long. 1991. *Introduction to Second Language Acquisition Research*. London: Longman.

Lasnik, H. 1989. On certain substitutes for negative data. In Matthews and Demopoulos (1989).

Lebeaux, D. 1990. The grammatical nature of the acquisition sequence: adjoin-alpha and the formation of relative clauses. In Frazier and de Villiers (1990).

Lee, D. 1992. Universal Grammar, learnability and the acquisition of L2 English reflexive binding by L1 Korean speakers. Unpublished doctoral dissertation, University of Southern California.

Leech, G. 1983. *Principles of Pragmatics*. London: Longman.

Levin, B., and M. Rappaport Hovav. 1995. *Unaccusativity: At the Syntax/Lexical Semantics Interface*. Cambridge, MA: MIT Press.

Levinson, S. 1983. *Pragmatics*. Cambridge: Cambridge University Press.

Li, C., and S. Thompson. 1976. Subject and topic: a new typology of language. In C. Li (ed.), *Subject and Topic*. New York: Academic Press.

Li, C., and S. Thompson. 1981. *Mandarin Chinese: A Functional Reference Grammar*. Berkeley, CA: University of California Press.

Lightfoot, D. 1991. *How to Set Parameters: Arguments from Language Change*. Cambridge, MA: MIT Press.

Lust, B. 1981. Constraints on anaphora in child language: a prediction for a universal. In Tavakolian (1981).

MacWhinney, B. (ed.). 1987. *Mechanisms of Language Acquisition*. Hillsdale, NJ: Lawrence Erlbaum.

Marantz, A. 1984. *On the Nature of Grammatical Relations*. Cambridge, MA: MIT Press.

Martohardjono, G., and S. Flynn. 1995. Language transfer: what do we really mean? In Eubank et al. (1995).

Matthews, R., and W. Demopoulos (eds). 1989. *Learnability and Linguistic Theory*. Dordrecht: Kluwer.

McDaniel, D., H. Cairns, and J. Hsu. 1990/1. Control principles in the grammars of young children. *Language Acquisition* 1: 297–335.

Meisel, J. (ed.). 1994. *Bilingual First Language Acquisition: French and German Grammatical Development*. Amsterdam: John Benjamins.

Menyuk, P. 1969. *Sentences Children Use*. Cambridge, MA: MIT Press.

Milsark, G. 1988. Singl-*ing*. *Linguistic Inquiry* 19: 611–34.

Müller, N. 1994. Parameters cannot be reset: evidence from the development of COMP. In Meisel (1994).

Munnich, E., S. Flynn, and G. Martohardjono. 1994. Elicited imitation and grammaticality judgment tasks: what they measure and how they relate to each other. In E. Tarone, S. Gass, and A. Cohen (eds), *Research Methodology in Second Language Acquisition*. Hillsdale, NJ: Lawrence Erlbaum.

Napoli, D. 1993. *Syntax: Theory and Problems*. Oxford: Oxford University Press.

Nishigauchi, T., and T. Roeper. 1987. Deductive parameters and the growth of empty categories. In Roeper and Williams (1987).

Nishimura, M. 1986. Intrasentential code-switching: the case of language assignment. In J. Vaid (ed.), *Language Processing in Bilinguals: Psycholinguistic and Neuropsychological Perspectives*. Hillsdale, NJ: Lawrence Erlbaum.

O'Grady, W., M. Dobrovolsky, and M. Aronoff (eds). 1989. *Contemporary Linguistics: An Introduction*. New York: St Martin's Press.

Oshita, H. 1995. Compounds: a view from suffixation and A-structure alteration. In G. Booij and J. van Marle (eds), *Yearbook of Morphology 1994*. Dordrecht: Kluwer.

Oshita, H. 1997. L2 acquisition of English unaccusative verbs: structural, crosslinguistic, and developmental aspects. Unpublished doctoral dissertation, University of Southern California.

Ouhalla, J. 1994. *Introducing Transformational Grammar*. London: Edward Arnold.

Perera, K., G. Collis, and B. Richards (eds). 1994. Growing Points in Child Language. Special issue of *Journal of Child Language* 21.

Pinker, S. 1984. *Language Learning and Language Development*. Cambridge, MA: Harvard University Press.

Pinker, S. 1989. *Learnability and Cognition*. Cambridge, MA: MIT Press.

Pollock, J.-Y. 1989. Verb movement, Universal Grammar, and the structure of IP. *Linguistic Inquiry* 20: 365–424.

Poplack, S. 1980/2. "Sometime I'll start a sentence in English *y termino en español*": toward a typology of code-switching. In J. Amastae and L. Elias-Olivares (eds), *Spanish in the United States: Sociolinguistic Aspects*. Cambridge: Cambridge University Press.

Poulisse, N. 1982. On the acquisition of *bring* and *take* by Dutch learners of English. *Interlanguage Studies Bulletin* 6: 109–27.

Quirk, R., S. Greenbaum, G. Leech, and J. Svartvik. 1985. *A Comprehensive Grammar of the English Language*. London: Longman.

Radford, A. 1988. *Transformational Grammar*. Cambridge: Cambridge University Press.

Radford, A. 1990. *Syntactic Theory and the Acquisition of English Syntax*. Oxford: Blackwell.

Radford, A. 1994. The syntax of questions in child English. In Perera et al. (1994).

Randall, J. 1992. The catapult hypothesis: an approach to unlearning. In Weissenborn et al. (1992).

Reuland, E., and A. Ter Meulen (eds). 1987. *The Representation of (In)definiteness*. Cambridge, MA: MIT Press.

Richards, M. 1976. *Come* and *go* reconsidered: children's use of deictic verbs in contrived situations. *Journal of Verbal Learning and Verbal Behavior* 15: 655–65.

Robison, R. 1990. The primacy of aspect: aspectual marking in English interlanguage. *Studies in Second Language Acquisition* 12: 315–30.

Robison, R. 1995. The aspect hypothesis revisited: a cross-sectional study of tense and aspect marking in interlanguage. *Applied Linguistics* 16: 344–70.

Roeper, T. 1987. The acquisition of implicit arguments and the distinction between theory, process, and mechanism. In MacWhinney (1987).

Roeper, T., and J. de Villiers. 1992. Ordered decisions in the acquisition of wh-questions. In Weissenborn et al. (1992).

Roeper, T., and E. Williams (eds). 1987. *Parameter Setting*. Dordrecht: Kluwer.

Rutherford, W. 1977. *Modern English*. 2nd edn. Vol. 2. New York: Harcourt Brace Jovanovich.

Rutherford, W. 1983. Language typology and language transfer. In S. Gass and L. Selinker (eds), *Language Transfer in Language Learning*. Rowley, MA: Newbury House.

Rutherford, W. (ed.). 1987a. *Language Universals and Second Language Acquisition*. Second edition. Amsterdam: John Benjamins.

Rutherford, W. 1987b. *Second Language Grammar: Learning and Teaching*. London: Longman.

Rutherford, W. 1989. Interlanguage and pragmatic word order. In Gass and Schachter (1989).

Sadock, J. 1971. Queclaratives. In *Papers from the Seventh Regional Meeting*. Chicago: Chicago Linguistics Society.

Schachter, J. 1989. Testing a proposed universal. In Gass and Schachter (1989).

Schwartz, B., and M. Gubala-Ryzak. 1992. Learnability and grammar reorganization in L2A: against negative evidence causing the unlearning or verb movement. *Second Language Research* 8: 1–38.

Seliger, H. 1989. Semantic transfer constraints on the production of English passive by Hebrew–English bilinguals. In Dechert and Raupach (1989).

Sharwood Smith, M. (1988). Imperfective versus progressive: an exercise in contrastive pedagogical linguistics. In W. Rutherford and M. Sharwood Smith (eds), *Grammar and Second Language Teaching: A Book of Readings*. New York: Newbury House.

Sheldon, A. 1977. On strategies for processing relative clauses: a comparison of children and adults. *Journal of Psycholinguistic Research* 6: 305–18.

Shi, D. 1990. The structure and interpretation of Chinese topic chain. Unpublished paper, University of Southern California.

Shi, D. 1993. Topic-prominent language and discourse-oriented language. Unpublished paper, University of Southern California.

Slobin, D. 1966. Grammatical transformations and sentence comprehension in childhood and adulthood. *Journal of Verbal Learning and Verbal Behavior* 5: 219–27.

Slobin, D. 1971. Developmental psycholinguistics. In W. Dingwall (ed.), *A Survey of Linguistic Science*. College Park: University of Maryland Linguistics Program.

Slobin, D. 1985. The child as linguistic icon-maker. In Haiman (1985).

Smith, D. 1978. Mirror images in Japanese and English. *Language* 54: 78–122.

Sorace, A. 1993. Incomplete vs. divergent representations of unaccusativity in non-native grammars of Italian. *Second Language Research* 9: 22–47.

Spencer, A. 1991. *Morphological Theory*. Oxford: Blackwell.

Sperber, D., and D. Wilson. 1986. *Relevance*. Oxford: Blackwell.

Stephany, U. 1992. Modality. In Fletcher and Garman (1992).

Stowell, T. 1980. Origins of phrase structure. Unpublished PhD dissertation, MIT.

Tai, J. 1985. Temporal sequence and Chinese word order. In Haiman (1985).

Tavakolian, S. (ed.). 1981. *Language Acquisition and Linguistic Theory*. Cambridge, MA: MIT Press.

Tenny, C. 1987. Grammaticalizing aspect and affectedness. Unpublished PhD dissertation, MIT.

Thomas, M. 1993. *Knowledge of Reflexives in a Second Language*. Amsterdam: John Benjamins.

Thompson, S. 1978. Modern English from a typological point of view: some implications of the function of word order. *Linguistische Berichte* 54: 19–35.

Traugott, E. 1989. On the rise of epistemic meanings in English: an example of subjectification in semantic change. *Language* 65: 31–55.

Vainikka, A. 1990. The status of grammatical default systems: comments on Lebeaux. In Frazier and de Villiers (1990).

Vendler, Z. 1967. *Linguistics in Philosophy*. Ithaca, NY: Cornell University Press.

Vergnaud, J.-R., and M.-L. Zubizarreta. 1992. The definite determiner in French and in English. *Linguistic Inquiry* 23: 595–652.

Wanner, E., and L. Gleitman (eds). 1982. *Language Acquisition: The State of the Art*. Cambridge: Cambridge University Press.

Weinberg, A. 1990. Markedness versus maturation: the case of subject–auxiliary inversion. *Language Acquisition* 1: 165–94.

Weissenborn, J., H. Goodluck, and T. Roeper (eds). 1992. *Theoretical Issues in Language Acquisition*. Hillsdale, NJ: Lawrence Erlbaum.

Wenzell, V. 1989. Transfer of aspect in the English oral narratives of native Russian speakers. In Dechert and Raupach (1989).

Wexler, K., and R. Manzini. 1987. Parameters and learnability in binding theory. In Roeper and Williams (1987).

White, L. 1985. The acquisition of parameterized grammar: subjacency in second language acquisition. *Second Language Research* 1: 1–17.

White, L. 1989. *Universal Grammar and Second Language Acquisition*. Amsterdam: John Benjamins.

White, L. 1990. Another look at the logical problem of foreign language learning: a reply to Bley-Vroman. *Linguistic Analysis* 20: 50–63.

White, L. 1991a. Adverb placement in second language acquisition: some effects of positive and negative evidence in the classroom. *Second Language Research* 7: 133–61.

White, L. 1991b. Second language competence versus second language performance: UG or processing strategies? In Eubank (1991a).

White, L. 1992. On triggering data in L2 acquisition: a reply to Schwartz and Gubala-Ryzak. *Second Language Research* 8: 120–37.

Whorf, B. 1956. *Language, Thought, and Reality: Selected Writings of Benjamin Lee Whorf*. Cambridge, MA: MIT Press.

Wolfram, W., and D. Christian. 1980. On the application of sociolinguistic information: test evaluation and dialect differences in Appalachia. In T. Shopen and J. Williams (eds), *Standards and Dialects in English*. Cambridge, MA: Winthrop.

Woolford, E. 1983. Bilingual code-switching and syntactic theory. *Linguistic Inquiry* 14: 520–36.

Yip, V. 1995. *Interlanguage and Learnability: From Chinese to English*. Amsterdam: John Benjamins.

Zobl, H. 1980. The formal and developmental selectivity of L1 influence on L2 acquisition. *Language Learning* 30: 43–57.

Zobl, H. 1987. Uniformity and source-language variation across developmental continua. In Rutherford (1987a).

Zobl, H. 1989. Canonical typological structures and ergativity in English L2 acquisition. In Gass and Schachter (1989).

Zobl, H., and J. Liceras. 1994. Functional categories and acquisition orders. *Language Learning* 44: 159–79.

Zwicky, A. 1970. Auxiliary reduction in English. *Linguistic Inquiry* 1: 323–36.

Index of Language

The languages listed are those, other than English, that figure in the textual material of the assignments (cited by number), and most frequently with reference to language-contact phenomena. The languages are indexed by assignment number.

General Index

All indexed items are referenced to the assignments in which they are introduced and/or discussed. Citations are therefore by assignment number (or letter, in the case of preliminary material), not page number.